Praise for Backroads and Backporches:
The Road Back to Me

DESIREE STEELE'S BOOK IS A FEARLESS JOURNEY through trauma, faith, and radical self-reclamation. Desiree writes with unflinching honesty about the messy, winding road to healing—offering not answers, but companionship for anyone who's ever had to rebuild themselves from the ground up.

*Michael Coleman, award-winning journalist and Communications Director for New Mexico Governor Michelle Lujan Grisham*

BACKROADS AND BACKPORCHES: THE ROAD BACK TO ME by Desiree Steele is so much more than your average autobiography—it's an invitation to pull up a chair and settle into an honest, often hilarious, sometimes heartbreaking conversation. Steele writes with the same authenticity she offers when you sit on her actual back porch—whether she's sharing tea, a treat, or a story, she brings her whole self, and in doing so, invites you to do the same. This is not a gratuitous retelling of a life, but a deeply reflective journey through trauma, love, faith, friendship, and the ongoing practice of finding oneself anew each day. As Steele beautifully reminds us, healing is not a destination; it's a journey of "learning how to carry grief in one hand and joy in the other, without dropping ourselves in the process." Blending memoir, poetry, and raw reflection, this quick but powerful read will have you reaching for a highlighter and a pen—because every few pages, you'll find a line that feels like it was written just for you.

*Dr. Christine Norton, LCSW-S, CCAT, CCTP, CET*

MOST MEMOIRS I'VE CHOSEN TO READ over the years have been entertaining, meaningful, and insightful. Never have I opened a biographical narrative to find myself so powerfully beckoned toward authentic living, to healing, to becoming more completely myself. Steele states early on that she hopes her readers might find her personal and spiritual insights relatable and get one to thinking. However, this reader certainly didn't expect to be highlighting on every page, making notes, and attempting to internalize the many consequential epigrams she offers. There's a term, self-actualization, used in psychology. I've done a great deal of self-reflection over my many decades but now see more clearly than I can go deeper, become even more whole. In fact, while turning each page, I longed to go deeper, facing even current pain. This book invites me to see the value in being more truthful with myself. Like many, I've grown and become "more me" because of moving through the hardest of times. But I still prefer to stuff, to numb, to power through. Steele's depth of reflection, revealing her own unwillingness to face the pain, pain which would not be pushed down, rang so very true. This book is not a lengthy treatise, but a conversation...one set on a cozy back porch or riding shotgun alongside her on a wandering back road.

*Carla Hays, MS, NBCC*

I'LL START BY SAYING THIS — I may be a little biased, because the author of this book is my cousin, but that doesn't change the truth: this book hit me deep.

From the very first page, Desiree's honesty grabs you. She doesn't sugarcoat anything or try to make her story neat and tidy — she tells it exactly how it was. It's raw, emotional, funny in the most unexpected places, and full of the kind of truth that only comes from surviving the hard stuff and choosing to heal anyway.

Reading this felt like sitting on the back porch with her, listening to stories that make you laugh one minute and tear up the next. I could feel her strength and vulnerability in every word. The way she talks about faith, pain, family, and finding her way back to herself is something I think a lot of people will connect with — even if they've never walked the same road.

What I love most is that she doesn't pretend healing is easy. She shows that it's messy, that it takes time, and that sometimes you have to face things you'd rather forget. But through all of it, there's this thread of hope and light that shines through.

Desiree's courage in writing this book — in sharing the parts of her story most people would keep hidden — is something I deeply admire. I'm so proud of her for turning pain into purpose and showing others that "easier doesn't heal," but truth does.

This book is real, it's brave, and it's absolutely beautiful.

*Darryl Carnley*
*Founder of My360Project*

I've watched Desiree fight her way through things most people never talk about out loud. Some of the roads she walked were forced on her—dark, painful, and far too heavy for a child. But she kept going. She kept choosing life, even when life didn't choose her back.

And then there were the roads she chose on her own. One of those roads was me! She chose me, and I chose her… and neither of us had a clue what that choice would demand or give. But 32 years later, I can tell you this: it was the best road I've ever taken!

I've seen her cry through sad days and dance through the happy ones. I've watched her rebuild herself piece by piece with a strength that still amazes me. She feels deeply, she carries more than most people will ever know, and yet she keeps on going, with heart, with grit, and a stubbornness that refuses to quit!

This book is Desiree—raw, brave, honest, and human. It's the story of a woman who refused to let her past define her and instead used it to live a life full of meaning. It isn't a perfect road, but it's hers… and she has walked it with courage!

I'm so proud of her! I'm proud of all the work she has put into our lives, and the work she has put into writing this book! Even though I've been there through so much of it, reading her words has really helped me see her in a new way, and I can't help but tear up with pride when I read it.

My prayer is that her story gives you real hope! Because if Desiree's journey teaches anything, it's that no matter where you start, no matter what life takes from you, you can still find your way back to yourself.

Bart Steele

# Backroads
## and
# Backporches
*the road back to me*

*Desiree Steele*

Published by:
Backroads and Backporches LLC
BackroadsandBackporches.com

Creative Direction & Editing:
NEWSBOY PUBLISHING
NewsboyPublishing.com

This is a work of non-fiction.

Copyright © 2025, Backroads and Backporches LLC
All rights reserved.

Published by: Backroads and Backporches LLC
www.BackroadsandBackporches.com

LIBRARY OF CONGRESS CATALOGING-IN-PUBLICATION DATA
Names: Steele, Desiree, author.
Title: Backroads and backporches : the road back to me / Desiree Steele.
Description:
Identifiers: LCCN: 2025926311 | ISBN: 979-8-9938726-1-2 (hardcover) | 979-8-9938726-0-5 (paperback) | 979-8-9938726-3-6 (ebook) | 979-8-9938726-2-9 (audio)
Subjects: LCSH Steele, Desiree. | Adult child sexual abuse victims--Biography. | Abused children –Biography. | Psychic trauma. | Mental healing. | Self-actualization (Psychology) | Photographers--Biography. | Texas--Biography. | BISAC BIOGRAPHY & AUTOBIOGRAPHY / Memoirs | BIOGRAPHY & AUTOBIOGRAPHY / Women | SELF-HELP / Personal Growth / Self-Esteem | BODY, MIND & SPIRIT / Inspiration & Personal Growth
Classification: LCC RC569.5.A28 S 2025 | DDC 616.8583690092--dc23

Creative Direction & Editing by Newsboy Publishing
Cover design by Newsboy Publishing
Book design by Newsboy Publishing

**NEWSBOY**
**PUBLISHING**
Buda, Texas
www.newsboypublishing.com

Cover photo and photos on pages 8, 103, 114, 124, 127, 131, 132, 133, 134, 153 by Desiree Steele, Backroads and Backporches LLC
Photo on pages 100, 101, 163, 173 by Michael Tarabay

# Contents

Before You Begin ..................................................................10

Prologue: Meet Me on My Backporch..................................13

Part One: The Roads of Childhood........................................19

Part Two: The Road That Led to Love..................................45

Part Three: The Roads of Friendship.....................................71

Part Four: The Roads of Faith and Self-Discovery............103

Part Five: The Roads Where the Light Shifted..................127

Part Six: The Roads of Resilience........................................137

Part Seven: The Backroads That Brought Me Home........153

Final Note From the Road....................................................167

# BEFORE YOU BEGIN…

If you picked up this book expecting it to be light and easy—well, it's not that kind of story.

It's raw.

It's real.

It has hope.

And it's mine.

I talk about Jesus, weed, healing, and a few things that might make some people uncomfortable. I cuss a little, laugh when it doesn't always seem appropriate, and promise to be as honest as I can, without the authorities being called on me.

You don't have to believe like me to read this. You don't even have to agree with me. But if you've ever been knocked down and had to find your way back up, you might find a piece of yourself somewhere in these pages.

Throughout this book, I mention moments that I later return to with more honesty and understanding. Some are painful, some are redemptive. I didn't write this story in order; I wrote it as I remembered it—how healing actually happens.

People have asked me, "Desiree, wouldn't it have been easier not to remember?"

Maybe.

But easier doesn't heal.

From ages two to eight, pieces of my life were tucked so far away that I didn't start remembering them until 2017. That first memory hit like a freight train I didn't see coming. The rest didn't start pouring out until after I healed from my second breast surgery, like my body and mind finally teamed up and said, "Alright, girl, you're safe. It's time to unpack the box."

If you're still reading, thank you for staying. All I ask is that you read with open hands and an open heart.

Because the backroads of my life are bumpy and messy, sometimes hilarious, and sometimes heartbreaking.

But every twist and turn leads me back to my back porch, where my truth finally gets to breathe.

———

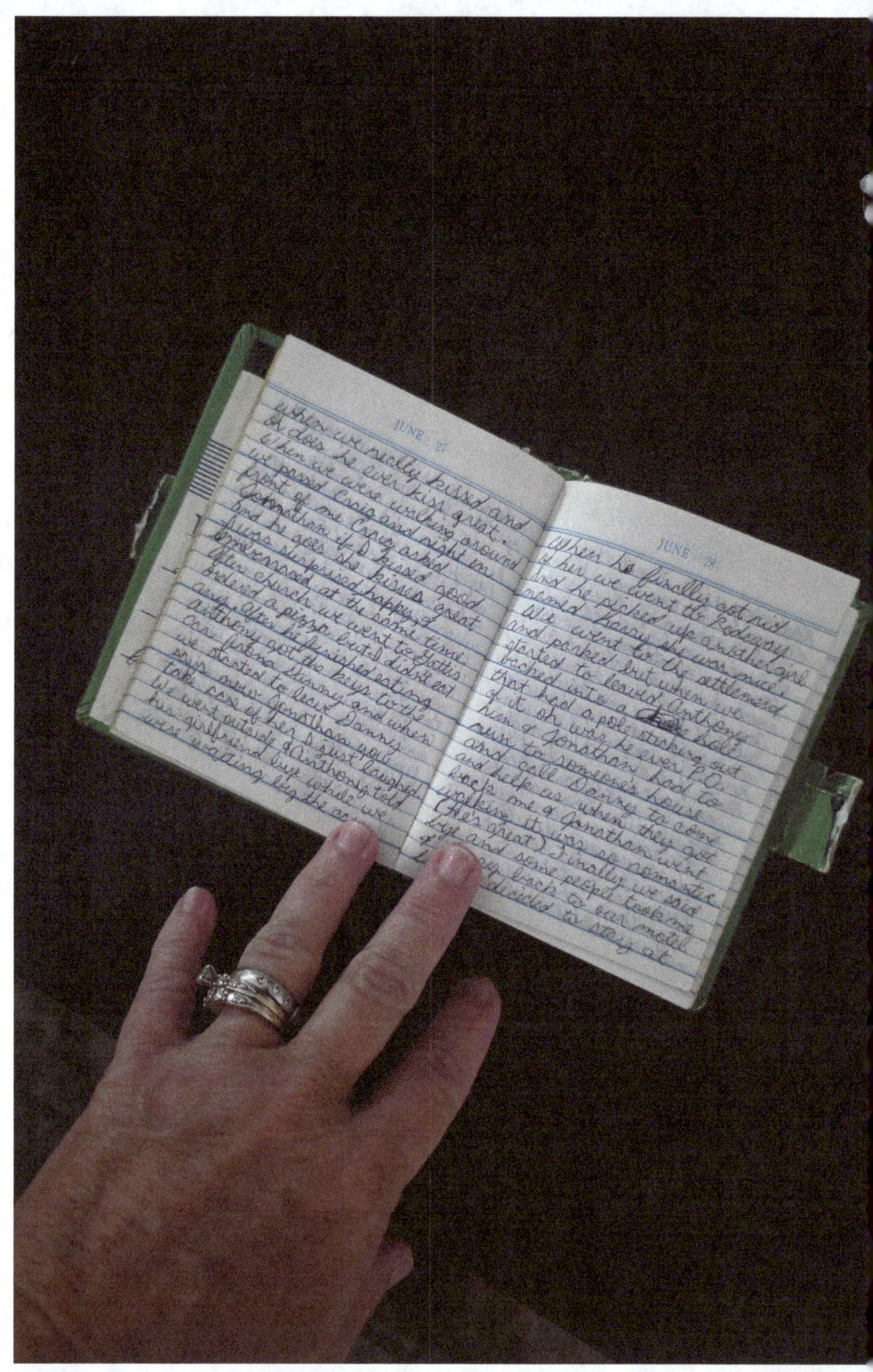

# Prologue: Meet Me on My Backporch

There's something honest about a back porch, and something freeing about a road.

Both are places where life slows down just enough for you to catch your breath, to pause, and to decide which way to go next. They're where truth shows up, quiet, raw, and uninvited, and if you sit still long enough, you can almost hear your heart exhale.

It's where the noise fades just enough for you to hear your own thoughts. It's where deep breaths come easier. Where your coffee cools slower, and time—if only for a moment—feels like it might actually be on your side. That's where I'm inviting you to meet me.
Not in a church pew. Not in a therapist's office. Not at a podium with answers neatly pressed and ready. But here, on my back porch—where I've cried, prayed, cussed, laughed, and talked about everything from raising kids to finding myself again after life flipped the script.

Eighteen years of homeschooling my kids taught me patience, grit, and how to improvise when the lesson plan, or life, went sideways. Somewhere along the line, after trauma, therapy, hormones that completely lost their minds, and discovering that a little weed can quiet the noise better than anything else I'd tried, I learned to lighten up. To laugh more. To stop trying to fix everything all the time and just let life be what it is—beautiful, messy, and mine.

I've sat on this porch with friends, swapping stories about the chaos of motherhood and the mystery of middle age, realizing that life doesn't stop handing out lessons—it just changes subjects. Sometimes we laugh our way through them, sometimes we limp—but we keep showing up.

What I've learned about pain is that it changes form. It doesn't stay where it started. It seeps into how you see yourself, how you show up in relationships, and how long you stare at a text before hitting send. It can silence you without saying a word.

And yet, healing has its own stubborn way of showing up, too.
It creeps in through honest conversations, small wins, held hands, and yes, sometimes even through writing a book that scares the hell out of you. Healing isn't tidy. It's messy, funny, exhausting, and worth every second of the work it takes.

This isn't a book about blame. It's not about revenge or regret. It's about taking my life back. It's about going back and gathering all the pieces of me I left behind, on sidewalks, in church pews, in old bedrooms and new cities, and finally letting them come home.

I've walked through seasons where I didn't know if I'd ever feel whole. And even now, wholeness feels more like a practice than a destination. But I know this much: I'm not the same woman I was when the road first cracked open in 2017.

I've spent decades learning how to carry grief in one hand and joy in the other, without dropping myself in the process.
And still, some mornings I wake up and forget what I know. Some nights I reach for old habits like they're a familiar blanket. But more often than not, I remember.

I remember who I am. I remember that my voice is mine now. My body is mine. My story—mine to tell.

This book won't give you a linear timeline. It won't tie up every thread with a bow. What it will do is walk you down the roads I've taken, the cracked ones, the backroads, the forgotten paths that still led somewhere.

You'll meet the girl who didn't know she was drowning. The teenager who found her voice in all the wrong places. The woman who rebuilt herself again and again, and the mother who tried to give her kids something better, even when she still felt broken. There's no guidebook for the kind of life I've lived. But maybe, just maybe, these pages will be a flashlight for someone else's dark night.

Maybe something in here will sit with you like a friend who doesn't need you to be okay.

So here I am.

I've pulled up a chair. The porch light is on. The road stretches out ahead.

I'm telling it all, not because I have to, but because I finally can.

And maybe, if you're carrying something heavy too, you'll find a little light on this road to guide you to your place of healing and peace.

We weren't made to walk it alone.

# The Road to Here

Before I ever wondered who I was or why I felt so different, I was just a kid with a spark, and a whole lot of questionable ideas I was more than willing to test out on the world. I didn't have a plan, but I had fire. And when you're five years old with fire in your belly and nobody explaining the rules in a language your little ears can fully hear, you make your own rules. You follow your own compass, even if it spins a little crooked.

I wasn't a wild child—I was just wired differently. Curious. Determined. Blunt. Fiercely loyal. Full of heart.

People loved me because I was adorable in my own lopsided way, tiny pigtails, coke-bottle glasses that magnified my eyes to cartoon size, a lisp that turned every word into something worth smiling at, and a bounce in my step that made it hard to stay mad at me for long. I was curious to a fault, always in motion, always asking questions I probably shouldn't. And even at that age, I knew I could be a little much. Cute and slightly annoying, a combination that somehow worked for me.

Some kids followed the path laid out for them. I was the kid on the side trail, collecting shiny rocks and climbing things I probably shouldn't. The one with chocolate on her face, questions in her mouth, and scraped-up knees. And even when things around me didn't make sense—when the adults weren't paying attention or when love came in strange shapes and short supply—I was still out there, turning over stones, pushing boundaries, and making my own kind of sense.

The truth is, I didn't grow up with clear answers. I grew up with contradictions. I had loud laughter and quiet sadness. I had moments of deep safety and stretches of being completely on my own—emotionally, spiritually, sometimes physically. I was seen and unseen, cherished and overlooked, all at once.

But what I had, what I always had, was the will to keep going. The will to find something good, even in the middle of the mess. That's the core of who I've always been.

This book isn't just about trauma, healing, faith, marriage, motherhood, or even loss—though it's all of those things.

It's about what it means to walk through life, lose your way, while finding a way back to yourself.

*Back to joy.*

*Back to love.*

*Back to peace*, even if just in moments.

*Back to God*, but not the God I was spoon-fed in childhood. The one I found in the quiet places. On backroads. On backporches. In the middle of heartbreak. In the middle of laughter. In the middle of being fully, imperfectly me.

Sometimes the roads we travel run side by side, two different paths that somehow lead to the same place. I've learned that more than one road can be right at the same time. One might be straight and familiar; the other, rough and full of detours. But if you pay attention, they'll both teach you something about grace, about timing, and about how home isn't a single destination—it's the place where your roads finally meet.

You won't find a straight line in these pages. What you'll find is the road—the real one and its mine. Winding and wide open, cracked and full of beauty, with pit stops, potholes, a few crashes, and handfuls of grace. You'll find the people who helped carry me and the ones who left me there bleeding. You'll find stories that will make you laugh out loud and others that might make you want to set something on fire.

Please don't.

And if you see parts of yourself in these pages, especially the messy parts, I hope you know this:

You're not broken.

You're not too much.

You're just on your road. And it's okay if it looks nothing like other people's. This is mine. These are the backroads and backporches that led me here.

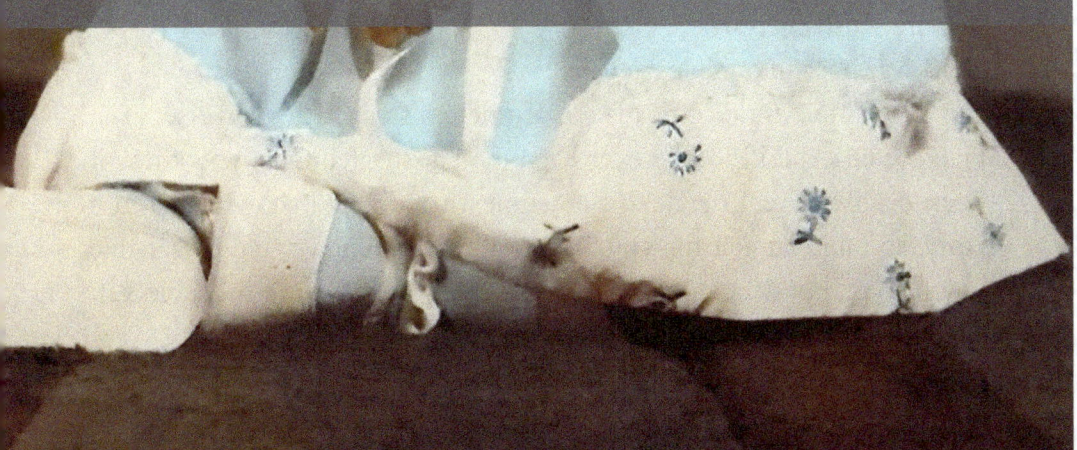

# Part One:
# The Roads of Childhood

## The In-Between

I was nearly two years old when my world finally came into focus. I sat cross-legged in front of our fish tank for the first time in my life. My mom said my nose practically pressed against the glass, staring like I'd just discovered buried treasure. I had just gotten my first pair of glasses, giant, round, coke-bottle lenses that swallowed my little face—and for the first time, I realized we had fish. Real, living, swimming fish that had been there all along. I sat there for hours, mesmerized. It wasn't that I didn't know the tank was there; I just hadn't seen it. Not really. For almost two years, the world had been a soft blur. Faces were shapes. Love was tone and touch. Life existed in fuzzy outlines, and I didn't even know what I was missing. And then, suddenly, I saw.

That moment says everything about my childhood. So much of it was like that—blurry until it wasn't. Things happening all around me, things I could feel but not name. And when they finally came into view, they hit hard. Like spotting fish that had been swimming beside you the whole time. Unseen, but always there.

No one chooses the road they're born onto. We just show up, mid-scene, in a story. Some land in the middle of love that wraps around us like a warm blanket. Some land in chaos. And some of us? We land somewhere in between soft in places, sharp in others, and never quite making sense everywhere else.

I was born into the in-between.

I was the third girl of the Turnell sisters. The surprise. The unexpected. And if you've ever been the unexpected One, you know it doesn't always feel magical. Sometimes it feels like showing up to a party no one planned for you. You walk in smiling, trying to act like you belong, but deep down you know—there's no seat at the table yet. You have to pull up your own chair and pour your own drink.

When I was born, and the doctor announced, "It's a girl," my mom

# The Roads of Childhood

cried. And not the sweet, overwhelmed-with-love kind of tears, they were more like "Oh, damn! Not another girl." But she didn't cuss, so it was probably just silence and a heavy sigh. She wanted a boy.

I grew up knowing that. Not because she said it over and over, but because it was just... there. Lingering. Tucked into moments and glances and jokes that weren't really jokes.

And then, as if being unexpected wasn't dramatic enough, I decided to cause a scene before I even left the nursery. My two grandfathers were standing outside the window, looking in at me, probably trying to make sense of yet another girl joining the mix, when they noticed I was turning blue. Panic set in. Nurses were called. My grandfathers placed their hands on that nursery window and started praying right then and there. The story goes they wouldn't stop, just prayed and cried and begged heaven to hold onto me. And I believe it did.

I came into this world knowing how to fight. Even before I had words, I was already pushing through, refusing to give up. Even if no one had made space for me, I was going to make my own space. I was a fighter from the beginning.

I wasn't unloved. I was very much loved, but it didn't always feel that way. And feelings? They're tricky like that.

That kind of shadow, being the one they didn't expect, sticks to you in quiet ways. Like being the only one missing from the photo. Or hearing your name followed by a sigh. Or being told to just be quiet for a minute—again.

But those weren't the only shadows. There were others—darker, heavier—the kind that settle over a child's life long before she knows how to name them—things no child should have to carry. Back then, I couldn't have explained them; I didn't have the language. But I knew the feeling: a sudden shrinking inside, an instinct to fold myself up small, a need to disappear before anyone noticed too much. I learned how to scan a room before stepping into it, to decide if I could breathe there or needed to stay on guard. At the time, I thought it was just my personality, this careful, watchful way of moving through the world. Later, I'd understand it for what it really was, survival training I never signed up for, taught long before I could tie my own shoes.

I was a curious kid. Loud, as in I never shut up. Constantly asking "why?" before I agreed to anything. That kind of kid who made Sunday School teachers second-guess their calling. And regular school teachers? Lord bless them. I wasn't trying to be difficult—I just didn't know how to fit inside boxes that were too small for me.

I felt things big. I asked too many questions. I noticed everything and didn't know how to hide it. And to top it off, I was nearly blind, hard of hearing, and had a speech impediment. Between the glasses, the questions, and the sugar I consumed daily, I was a lot. A lovable lot, but still... a lot.

And yes, I also ate way too much candy, to the point that my teeth were literally rotting. Sugar was comfort. Control. My personal stash of sweetness in a world that didn't always feel soft. I probably had cavities in teeth I hadn't even grown yet.

I was also a world-class hider. Closets, cabinets, under beds—you name it. If it had a door, I was behind it. My mom always said I could vanish like magic at any family gathering.

One time, during a dinner party, she went searching for me and my little friend, okay... boyfriend, and found us tucked in a closet. She opened the door, looked at me with *that mom face*, and said, "Now Desiree... what are you doing?" Innocently (the jury is still out on that one) looking up at her with a stare, I answered, "I eat a peanup (not a typo, that's how I said it), and then I kiss him. I eat another peanup, then I kiss him again." I was five.

What can I say? I liked boys early. And peanuts.

# Independence

I liked the idea of being independent before I could even tie my shoes or ride a bike. Determined was the polite word for it. The truth? I was just plain stubborn. Once I set my mind to something, there was no talking me out of it, especially if it meant proving I could do what the grown-ups did.

Case in point: I was four when I decided I was going to make my own food. My cousin Jamie and I were out in Terlingua, where our families went hunting. If you've ever been out there, you know. It's the kind of place where the dirt sticks under your nails, the wind never stops blowing, and when the sun drops, and that desert cold cuts straight through you when the sun fades. But we figured if the adults could do it, so could we. Armed with a .22 rifle (yep, people actually trusted kids with those back then) and the kind of confidence only kids have, we went rabbit hunting. Before long, we had one. Feeling mighty proud, we skinned it, hung it up like we'd seen the grown-ups do with deer, and the next day we cut off the meat and threw it into a cast-iron skillet over the fire.

Now, you might be thinking, "That's impressive for a four- and six-year-old." And it might've been—if it hadn't been completely disgusting. No butter, no seasoning, nothing but sad, gray chunks of boiled rabbit floating in water. One bite was all it took for me to decide I was done. Jamie ate his because we'd been taught, "If you kill it, you eat it." But I spit mine right out. We might've been tough little West Texas kids, but no amount of grit could make that rabbit taste right.

# Saved By a Pringles Can

And then there was the time I tried to save a soul… with a Pringles can. Some kids play house. Some kids collect bugs. And then there was me. My cousin Jamie (my accomplice in all my big adventures and memories) convinced me that we were on a mission to save a neighbor's soul from eternal damnation.

We lived in a fourplex in Fairbanks, Alaska, with a rooftop balcony above us, where our neighbor was growing a little garden, not of vegetables, but of marijuana. My cousin, always the idea man, convinced me that it was our mission to get rid of the devil leaves he was growing in his nefarious rooftop garden. So, like two tiny vigilantes, we snuck onto his rooftop while he was out, plucked every last bit of the "contraband," and stuffed it into empty Pringles cans. We then weighed them down with rocks and took a nice stroll to the local leech-filled pond, where we launched the cans into the depths of its belly.

*Problem solved. Soul saved.*

Except that the neighbor didn't exactly see it that way. When he realized his entire stash was gone, he stormed downstairs, yelling at our dads, demanding to know what had happened. Of course, my cousin took the blame; everyone already knew he was the mastermind behind most of our trouble, but I stood right there beside him, a five-year-old accomplice, certain we had done the right thing. Looking back, maybe that was part of the same instinct I'd been quietly sharpening since I was little, scanning for danger, deciding who was safe and who needed "saving," even if I got it wildly wrong sometimes.

## The Long Road to a Little Confidence

Let's fast forward to sixth grade. I'd traded pigtails for a little more sass and a lot more confidence. By then, I liked to think of myself as pretty tough, quick with a comeback, fast with my feet when I needed to be. I wasn't scared of much, but there were still a few people who could cut straight through that armor.

One of them was this kid from school, a mean little shit who seemed to wake up every morning thinking, "How can I ruin Desiree's day?" He didn't just pick on me; he stalked me like it was his personal sport. One afternoon, I was riding my bike home when I heard it—the sharp, ugly sound of metal clinking behind me. I glanced over my shoulder and there he was, pedaling hard, swinging a heavy chain. Before I could swerve, the chain cracked across my face, knocking my glasses clean off. I remember watching them fly, skidding across the pavement. Later, when I picked them up, I saw the chip in the lens—a permanent reminder of that day.

I wasn't mad. I was just… sad. Glasses were expensive, and we didn't have money for another pair. Those glasses were my lifeline, and now they were damaged. And yeah, I was scared too—not just because of what he did, but because I knew there wasn't a damn thing I could do about it. I never told my parents. I just took the long way home from then on. Not because I was weak, but because I wasn't stupid. Some fights aren't worth it. Survival isn't about winning; it's about knowing how to keep going. I'd been in that training program for years—always reading the signs, figuring out when to stand my ground and when to take the long way home. And I always did.

I wore those busted glasses, with that chip in the lens, until the day I was at my cousin's house. We were riding his homemade go-kart, one of those rattling contraptions pieced together from whatever scraps were lying around. I was hanging onto the back when he slammed on

# The Roads of Childhood

the brakes. Next thing I knew, I was airborne. I landed hard, and those already-battered glasses didn't survive. I picked them up, bent and broken, and my dad just looked at me and said, "Well, I guess it's time you got contacts." I could've hugged him right then. Finally, no more "four eyes." With those contacts came a little more confidence, which I was going to need for what came next.

But even in the chaos of it all—feeling too much, seeing too little, sugar-high and hiding—I wasn't totally alone. Not completely. There were people who saw me, even if they didn't always understand me. There were places that felt like refuge—porches, creeks, the patch of shade under a big oak, or the corners of noisy rooms where nobody noticed I was quietly paying attention. And there were moments—small, fleeting—where I felt held. Even just for a second.

That's the thing about childhood. It's not just one thing. It's layers. Some are clear, some are cloudy. Some are loud and messy, others are so quiet they almost slip by unnoticed. And the road you're born onto? It may be cracked, confusing, wild—but eventually, you learn how to walk it. Sometimes barefoot. Sometimes sideways. But you walk it. And if you're lucky, you find a place, or a person, that gives you just enough breath to keep going. A pause in the chaos. A soft place to land. Those became my safe havens. And I'll never forget them.

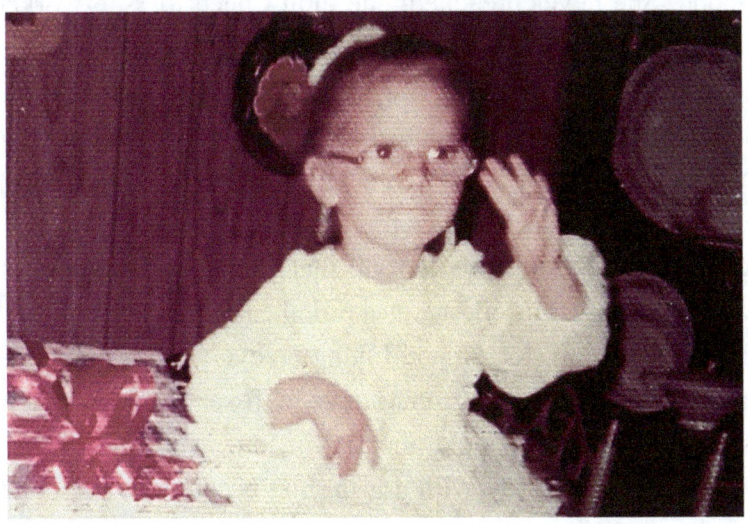

## The Roots That Held Me

If I could bottle up the feeling of home, it wouldn't be the house I grew up in that was always changing. It would be my Grandmama and Grandad Turnell's porch on a slow summer afternoon.

I'm little, legs sticking straight out because they don't reach the step below, sitting on the top porch step with a dented metal bowl in my lap, snapping green beans. Grandmama is next to me, humming a hymn so soft it almost blends in with the buzz of cicadas. Every so often, the wind moves through her flowers, and I swear even the marigolds pause to listen. She doesn't say much—she never had to. Her presence says everything I need to hear: You're wanted here. You belong here. The world can spin and break out there, but here, you can breathe.

Her house wasn't fancy, but it was steady. It had a rhythm that made sense. The garden out back was always alive with something growing. The kitchen always carried the smell of life—fresh tomatoes on the counter, bread rising under a dish towel, and the faint trace of morning coffee. Grandmama didn't just grow vegetables; she grew a sense of belonging. Her way of loving was quiet, but it went all the way to the bone. She never preached; she didn't need to. She worked. She nurtured. She hummed. She taught me to tend without words—how to soften the soil, watch for new growth, and trust that patience brings life. Granddad was the other side of that world—big, booming, and unforgettable. His laugh could shake the walls, and his voice in prayer seemed to rise straight to heaven. It startled me sometimes, but the second he pulled me into his lap, all that sound became comfort. His arms were a fortress. His chest was a drumbeat I could lean on.

He loved telling stories, and I hung on every word. I can still hear him talking about one of our ancestors—a Texas Ranger who worked alongside the Choctaw people and fell in love with one of the "little women there," as he'd say with a grin. She became part of our family line.

# The Roads of Childhood

Then came the story that still gives me goosebumps. He said that one Sunday, in a tiny Nazarene church in Placid, Texas, a little white girl stood up and began to worship in fluent Choctaw. She had never spoken a word of it before, yet there she was, praising in the language of our ancestors. "That," he said, "was the day our family came to know Jesus."

Even as a kid, I felt the power in that story—the way faith, connection, and history were all braided together in one beautiful moment.

Their house didn't have a TV, but it had treasures, stacks of National Geographic magazines. I'd sprawl on the rug, flipping through glossy pages, staring at faces from around the world. People who looked nothing like me, living lives I couldn't imagine. Maybe that's where my love for stories began, right there, in their living room, with the smell of bread baking and the sense that I was safe enough to dream beyond my own little world.

Even now, when life gets too loud, I go there in my mind. I feel the rough porch step under my legs. I smell the bread in the oven. I hear Grandmama humming and Granddad laughing. That place, those people—they were my roots. They held me steady when nothing else could. And I carry them with me still.

The Roads of Childhood

# Hiding in Plain Sight

Before I ever understood what I was doing, I was hiding. Not out of rebellion or mischief, but out of instinct. I had a whole rotation of secret spots: behind the couch, tucked in closets, wedged beneath the bed. That space under the bed was my favorite. It felt like my own secret world, where shadows offered shelter and silence didn't ask questions. I think I even got in trouble a few times for disappearing too often. But I wasn't trying to be bad—I was just trying to breathe. To find a space where I didn't feel like I was in the way.

When the quiet corners weren't enough, I built my own. I imagined new worlds where I was the mom, the protector, the one who stayed. I clung to anyone who gave me a scrap of attention, sometimes good people, sometimes not. I thought kindness meant safety. It took me a long time to learn that wasn't always true.

There was this doll, Christie. Big, red hair you could pull long or short. I mothered her the way I had seen it done, fed her invisible bottles, tucked her in tight, made her little homes out of blankets and leftover boxes. We had picnics on the carpet and adventures in the quiet corners of my mind.

The old shed in the backyard became our castle, our church, our store, whatever I needed it to be. We made mud pies, carved out hillside beds, and built entire towns with cousins and neighborhood kids. None of it lasted past the next rain, but in those fleeting moments, I felt free.

Even now, I know it wasn't just pretend. That wasn't just play. It was survival. I was creating a space where I could belong, a place that made more sense than the one I'd been handed.

I didn't always feel unseen. But maybe I was. Or maybe that's just how it was in the 70s and 80s. We were all latchkey kids, all a little forgotten. We let ourselves in after school, made our own snacks, and knew better than to interrupt the adults unless someone was bleeding. None of my friends had helicopter parents. We were the generation of figuring it out. We existed in the gaps.

# My Momma

My momma was magnetic. Not in the try-hard, look-at-me way, but effortlessly, jaw-droppingly magnetic. Stunningly beautiful. Incredibly talented at just about everything she touched. She lit up a room when she walked in—and I swear, even now, nearing 80, she still does.

There was always laughter around her. Loud, full-belly, throw-your-head-back laughter. She was the woman with bold lipstick or no makeup at all, whichever fit the moment. She didn't just host holidays—she produced them. Our living room could have passed for a Southern Living spread during Christmas. There were lights strung everywhere, candles flickering on every surface, and gifts that somehow made you feel like she had read your soul.

She was the kind of mom who gave me the birds-and-the-bees talk while driving to Polar Bear Ashburn for ice cream—mid-scoop, mid-shock. She thought it was hilarious to hire an Air Force stripper for my 18th birthday. I was slightly embarrassed but also thrilled. I mean, who doesn't love a man in uniform? She had a way of making even the weirdest or most awkward moment into a story people would repeat for years. That was her magic. Warm, generous, unforgettable. A little chaotic. A little wild. Always bold.

But behind all that sparkle, there was also sadness. I still remember the day I came home from kindergarten and found her passed out on the stairs. It was the first time I saw my momma completely undone, and even though I didn't have the words back then, something in me knew—not everything was okay.

# Backroads and Backporches

Even as a little girl, I could feel it. That subtle tension in the air. That buzzing undercurrent that made me study the room, measure people's moods before I spoke. I don't think I ever truly relaxed. Not all the way. I didn't feel fully seen. Fully safe. Fully... settled. There was love. I never doubted that. But I didn't always know where I fit inside the beautiful, chaotic world she created. Maybe that's when the real hiding started. Not in the closets or behind furniture—but inside myself. I clung to the laughter and the lights, but I also became skilled at holding my breath through the parts that felt too unpredictable.

Now, when I look back, I carry both sides of that childhood: the joy and the ache. The magic and the tension. The stories we told at the table, and the silence I learned to sit in alone. Because even with all that beauty, home wasn't a place where I could fully exhale.

## The Roads of Childhood
# My Daddy
---

My daddy was quiet. Not the gruff, mean kind of quiet, just off in his own world most of the time, or away working. I don't have a ton of memories of him being around when I was little, but I do have one that stuck.

I was seven, and still riding a bike with training wheels. The teasing had already started. Kids can be cruel when they smell your insecurity. But that day, he knelt, adjusted the seat, held the back, and said, "You're ready." He ran alongside me, hand steady, until—he wasn't there anymore. I was riding. On my own. And when I looked back and saw him smiling, it felt like more than just balance—I had his attention. Just for a moment, I had him.

## Backroads and Backporches

But life didn't offer many of those moments.

I remember my twelfth birthday, and the strawberry cake never even made it to the table. My parents got into a fight, and that pretty pink cake ended up painting the ceiling with pink icing and sweet cake. That image burned into my memory like a metaphor. And not long after my twelfth birthday, things shifted again.

We were sitting in my parents' bedroom, my two sisters and I. I don't remember my mom being there, but I can still see the desk. That desk sat in the corner, and that's where he was when he told us he was leaving. He didn't yell. He didn't cry. He just… said it. As a matter of fact. Like it was something simple. Like it wouldn't shatter us. When the words settled into the room like dust, I stood up and walked out the front door. I didn't make a scene. I didn't ask questions. I just wandered the neighborhood and cried until my chest hurt. I was twelve, and my heart already knew what it meant to hold pain quietly. He left.

To this day, I get emotional on my birthday. I'll find myself needing space or fighting back tears I can't quite name. It's like my body remembers what my mind has learned to pack away.

# Becoming Me

As I moved into my teen years, the hiding changed. I wasn't crawling under beds or ducking into closets anymore—I was shrinking in plain sight. I learned how to wear the right smile, say the right thing, laugh at the right time. I became a master at looking fine while feeling anything but.

But even in the quiet, I was building something. A quiet strength. A voice I would one day learn to use. And I was beginning to understand that the roads that shaped me didn't just carry heartache—they carried grit, creativity, tenderness, and a deep understanding of what it means to feel. That little girl who used to hide wasn't weak. She was surviving. She was watching. She was becoming.

# Teen Years – Messy, Loud, and Mine

The night of my 13th birthday party is frozen in my memory like a little bubble of magic. We were living in a duplex, and my mom threw the party in our carport, nothing fancy, but to me, it felt like a ballroom. There was a cookie cake, music, and a string of lights that transformed our little space into a teenage dream. My friends danced like the world was ours, and for that night. I felt pure, unshakable joy. Even now, that night sticks with me because it reminded me of something simple and true: my mom showed up big for me that birthday, just like she did for all my birthdays, even when things were hard. Her love was always there, and it came in many forms.

After that year in the Richie Rich neighborhood, also known as the Westlake area of Austin, we moved north of the river, where we felt more at home. It was the kind of place where single moms raised wild kids who had barely any rules, and thankfully, none of us ended up in juvy. I still have friends from that wild-west chapter, where guys, and a few girls, would duke it out in the local park after school like they were the Von Erich brothers or Sugar Ray Leonard. We had no rules, but damn, we had fun.

I don't go deep into my teen years in this book, but that doesn't mean the stories aren't there. Big hair. Bad decisions. Dance floors sticky with spilled beer. Lake nights that smelled like sunscreen and bonfire smoke. Fake IDs that fooled exactly no one. Stolen beers from neighbors' fridges when we thought we were smooth. We were hoodlums, and thank God there were no cell phones or social media. No evidence. Just memories and a few hazy photographs that somehow survived.

But before all that came the summer before ninth grade, when I made one of the hardest decisions of my life: I moved in with my dad full-time.

## Backroads and Backporches

My parents had divorced when I was younger, and I'd always lived with my mom. She was strong, composed, whip-smart, a woman who didn't need to raise her voice to make her point. But we were oil and water. Or maybe we were just mirrors, too much alike in ways that rubbed each other raw.

As much as I loved her, I needed something different. I had started going to church, craving structure and stability, something that made sense, something that could anchor me. At the time, my dad was the one who could give me.

I knew it crushed her when I left to live with him. She didn't beg me to stay, but her silence was heavy with disappointment. It hung between us like thick summer air, and I could feel it every time we locked eyes. That decision marked a turning point between us. We always loved each other, but the closeness we had once built took years to find its way back.

Life with my Dad was a different world. He wasn't one for long talks, but his love was steady. He was present. Consistent. Our home became the go-to spot for my friends. He cooked for all of us and then some, tossed chili pequins into people's mouths for laughs, and took us out on his boat. Friday nights meant movie rentals, and Saturday mornings meant chocolate-covered donuts. That quiet care changed me. It gave me space to breathe and to just be.

Freshman year, I switched to a private Christian school in South Austin. The hope was that it would keep me out of trouble. For a while, it did. I memorized the scriptures, sang in chapel, and tried to do the "right thing." But it didn't take long before I started feeling like I didn't belong. Not because of God. I never stopped believing in Him. It was the people, the pressure, and the way things were handled. Truth is, I didn't leave that church. I was pushed out. Or at least that's how it felt. By sophomore year, we moved back up north, and I was right back in the chaos of public school. My crew hadn't changed. We skipped class, cried over boys, and made dumb choices in the backs of trucks. It was wild, it was messy, and it was mine.

# The Roads of Childhood

My sisters were woven through it all. We didn't fight, because it wasn't allowed. But we had our own ways of communicating, and we always had each other's backs. We cheered, we roasted, we warned each other about deadbeat friends. There were nights we would walk into a club and the DJ or band would yell, "The Turnell sisters are here!" The men noticed us. The women either joined us or talked about us. But we weren't mean. We let everyone in—unless you crossed us. When we stood together, you didn't mess with us.

One night, I'll never forget, when I was sixteen, I woke from a nightmare that shook me to my core. I hadn't remembered all of my trauma yet, not fully. That wouldn't come for another 40 years, but something came through that night. I walked quietly into my dad's room, unsure if I belonged there at that age. I just needed him. I slipped under the covers, and without a word, he reached over and patted my back. Slow. Gentle. Steady. That simple gesture healed something in me. It told me I was safe. Loved. Seen.

Looking back, those years were a mix of bruises and blessings, heartbreak and hallelujahs. I didn't realize it then, but every messy, beautiful moment was teaching me something about love, trust, and who I was becoming. I was learning what safety felt like, what it didn't, and how much strength it takes to keep choosing both grace and grit when life keeps throwing curveballs. I was far from figuring it all out—but even then, the road was already shaping me into the woman I'd one day become.

# Lessons from Childhood

**1. Trust your gut.**
If something doesn't feel right, it probably isn't. That little whisper inside you? It's there for a reason. Listen to it, or at least proceed with caution.

**2. Imagination is a beautiful gift.**
It's what kept my heart and spirit young, helping me escape when I needed to. But it can also blur reality, turning shadows into monsters or people into saints. It's both a sanctuary and a trickster.

**3. You can have both a good and tough childhood.**
Life isn't all black and white. Some people can wound you deeply and still hold moments of love. You can love them, but you can also protect yourself—with boundaries that keep your peace intact.

**4. Outside is where all things get better.**
The world feels lighter under open skies. Fresh air, dirt under your feet, and a little sunshine can heal things no doctor or preacher ever could.

**5. Kids learn in all kinds of ways.**
I wasn't a traditional learner. They called me slow, sometimes even dumb. But I just saw the world differently. I hate very few things, but being put in a box is one of them.

*Maybe the things that made us different as kids weren't flaws at all—they were clues, quietly pointing us toward who we were always meant to be.*

# Part Two: The Road That Led to Love

## The Road That Should Have Ended Me

If you've ever wondered how one decision can change the entire direction of your life, let me take you to a dark backroad in September of 1992.

Some roads take us exactly where we're meant to go. Others are detours, rough, rocky paths we probably should've skipped. And then there are the roads that should have ended us—but didn't.

I was drinking hard, partying harder, and doing my best to stay numb. My parents thought I was an alcoholic. One of my guy friends even called my sister and said, "She's not doing good. I'm worried about her." And he was right to be worried.

That September, I wrecked my truck driving home from a bar. Drunk. Alone. Reckless.

That night should've killed me. I don't say that for drama—I say it because it's the truth.

I'd left the bar with a heavy heart. A guy I'd been seeing had left with another girl, and seeing them together knocked the wind out of me. I was hurt, mad, and stupid enough to get behind the wheel anyway. He happened to have been behind me, and later said something told him to follow. He watched my headlights disappear around a bend, and then saw my truck flip, end over end—three times.

When the world finally stopped spinning, the silence was deafening. I sobered up in the flips. I opened my eyes to glass glittering across the dashboard, twisted metal around me, and the smell of dirt and gasoline in the air. Not one cut. Not one bruise. Not a single broken bone. Just a broken nail, "Shit. Shit! Shit!" coming from my mouth, and a heart pounding so loud it felt like something bigger than me was knocking.

# The Road That Led to Love

    I climbed out with shaking hands and an overwhelming sense that I'd just been handed a miracle. I shouldn't have walked away from that night—but I did.

    In the quiet days that followed, something inside me shifted. A whisper I hadn't heard in years stirred up again. I turned back toward the faith I'd always longed for but had been running from.

Back then, I thought that meant getting back to church, because that's all I knew. I didn't yet understand that God can meet you right in the wreckage. In your apartment. On the bathroom floor. On a back porch at 2 a.m.

    I remember sitting in my room one night not long after the wreck, journal open, hands still trembling, writing, "God, if you're real, and you still want me, I want you too." No altar. No choir. No fancy prayer. Just me, a pen, and a life I wasn't willing to throw away anymore.

I did go back to church, and I was met with kindness, though sometimes it came with strings. People have stipulations. That's why I've always loved God and dogs the most—because they both meet you exactly where you are: messy, shaken, and still somehow grateful.

    I didn't know it then, but someone was already headed down my backroad.

## The Call on Christmas Eve

---

A few months after the wreck, it was Christmas Eve. I was still raw, still piecing myself back together, but something in me had shifted. My phone rang.

It was Bart.

We hadn't spoken in years. He was living in Virginia, and I was in Texas. That night, while visiting family, he picked up the phone—nudged by a mutual friend who apparently talked him into it. I owe that friend a beer and probably my marriage.

When I heard Bart's voice, something in me lit up. The armor I'd built—the sarcasm, the edge, the defiance softened.

I invited him over. He came.

When he walked in, it wasn't dramatic. It was easy, like slipping into a favorite old sweatshirt. My sisters were there. My mom was there. It was chaotic and funny and light. The kind of night that feels like nothing and everything at the same time.

Under all the laughter and teasing, something important cracked open. I didn't fully understand it, but I knew I wanted someone who understood my love for God—and there he was. He didn't compete with that part of me. He just let it be.

As he got up to leave, I walked him to the door. When it closed, I turned to my mom and sisters and said, "I'm going to marry him someday."

They looked at me like I'd lost my mind. One laughed, "Oh God, Desiree—not again." I didn't laugh back. I knew.

It wasn't a fairytale. No movie montage. Just something solid I hoped would be real.

Everything can change in one phone call.

# The Road That Led to Love

## Choosing Each Other

---

Falling in love with Bart wasn't fireworks—it was an unfolding. A slow realization that here was someone who wouldn't make me fight to be chosen. Someone who didn't leave. Someone who didn't flinch when I showed up with my full self, trauma, sass, silence, fire, and all.

Still, I brought old instincts, ready to defend, ready to earn love I already had. It took years to learn I didn't have to fight with him the way I'd fought with everyone else. But patterns show up, and mine did often.

Many times over the next 34 years, I'd walk out—never forever. I mean the kind of "walk out" where I got in the car, drove to a coffee shop, cried into a sugary drink, and came home. Back then, I didn't understand why. Now I know—I needed space for emotions too heavy to carry inside four walls.

With him, I didn't have to perform—though I did. I didn't have to hide—though I did. I could just be. That was new.

We both brought our own language. My CPTSD, ADHD, and dissociation made communication hard. Sometimes I'd shut down, drift out, or miss the cues. Bart had his own wiring that didn't always line up with mine. Subtlety wasn't his strength; emotions weren't always mine. We spoke different dialects of love and kept trying anyway.

There were nights I cried because I couldn't find the words. Days he went quiet and I thought he didn't care—when he was actually overwhelmed and caring deeply. The odds haven't been stacked in our favor. Marriage with childhood wounds is anything but simple.

But here we are—because we chose patience, humor, and each other.

I've always carried a picture of us on a porch swing, surrounded by family. A legacy. Strong? We've nailed that. Healthy? That part's still under review. Little by little, the walls come down.

Then love required bottles, budgets, and backup plans.

## Parenthood

I wanted to be a mom more than anything. I read the books and took the classes, thinking that if I prepared enough, I could "get it right." Truth: parenting from brokenness never lands clean. I parented out of protection and fear, trying to look like I had it together. Some things worked. Some didn't. I wouldn't know how badly until later.

We didn't always agree. I leaned into emotion and instinct (and fear more than I like to admit). Bart was steady, logical, and structured. I navigated by feeling; he navigated by "get it done." We met in the middle for our kids and our sanity.

Bart trusted me so much that he basically gave me free rein. He was the fun one—the "favorite parent." I carried the heavier weight—making calls, holding the fear of getting it wrong. It was lonely at times, but we balanced each other. Looking back, we both wish he'd been more involved early, and I wish I'd loosened my grip sooner.

Somehow, all three turned out to be good humans anyway. I tried not to push perfection on them, but I still made mistakes. That's parenting. In today's world, it's hard as hell.

Thank goodness my kids didn't have social media as littles. We had sensible rules: freedom inside boundaries; mess up, and it affects all of us. They pushed limits once they were grown, which opened my eyes to new ideas and ways of living. The checklist approach doesn't work. What did work: consistency, honesty, grace, and boundaries with room to breathe.

Parenthood softened us in places we didn't know needed softening. We were sleep-deprived, overwhelmed, head-over-heels in love, and sometimes hanging by a thread. We learned to communicate without words. A glance at 2 a.m. A handoff when we were out of answers. Silent teamwork over budget spreadsheets. We fought over ridiculous things and cried over tiny victories. The everyday showing up reshaped us. It made us us.

## Backroads and Backporches

There's an intimacy in raising kids that isn't romantic but feels deep. Someone has seen you at your worst, messy bun, cracked nipples, pacing with a screaming baby, and still chooses you.

## Our Babies

Breanna - Bre, because it's easier than correcting people forever. My guinea pig child (I've apologized a thousand times). The loudest of our three quiet kids. Tenacious in school. A precious soul with words that could change the world. Her childhood favorite was Francesco's Friendly World about caring for creation; she became an environmental engineer.

Noah - born barely breathing. He caught up with a booming voice like my Grandad, a stubborn streak, and the courage to ditch football for theater. Open-hearted and romantic, a gifted actor and singer. The most like me in a lot of ways. He once wrote me a song; it's my forever number-one.

Skyler - Sky, the baby with an old-soul streak. Fiercely independent and creative. Selling art since she was four. Sees the world differently, like her dad. At ten, she read an organic gardening book and designed our backyard garden. Needed freedom outside traditional school—and thrived.

All three went to college on their own steam. All three are rock climbers. All three love their momma.

Watching Bart with our adult kids has been its own joy. He may not always connect emotionally the way I want, but he's steady. He's a good place to land. That's the best kind of dad.

Parenthood didn't just grow our family; it deepened our marriage. Not perfectly. Not painlessly. But deeply.

Showing up every day reshaped us—changed us to the core.

Backroads and Backporches

# The Oak and the Wildflower

---

I've never fit a mold. I'm a wildflower.
Wildflowers don't grow in tidy rows. Their seeds scatter with the wind, carried by rain or caught in a bird's beak, and they bloom wherever they land, in meadows, cracks in the pavement, places no one expects. That's me.

Maybe some of that came from trauma, the scattering, the searching for safe ground. But mostly, it's just who I am. Honest. Faithful. Unafraid of change. I shift, I grow, I surprise people—sometimes even myself. I don't stay too long anywhere… except in Bart's arms. He's my one and only—the only one I want to hold me.

Now, for those who try to read between the lines, no, I've never cheated on my husband. Let's just clear that up. I'm flighty, not flaky. My spirit wanders, but my loyalty doesn't. My mind might take the scenic route, but my heart always finds its way back home. Always back to him.

Bart is an oak—roots sunk deep, steady through every storm. Sometimes that steadiness makes me restless, but the truth is, I need his roots as much as he needs my wild. He tries to ground me, and over time, he's learned to respect the way I bloom. I may drift, but I always come back to the oak. He is home.

One Saturday after the farmer's market, after a week of butting heads, I felt that familiar pull to run. Instead, I chose gratitude. I started small. Thank God for my bed. Then another thing, and another. Gratitude shifts things, even when nothing else will.

We still spark. I once asked him what he loved most about me. Without missing a beat, he said, "How brave you are. You let the sunshine come out of you, no matter who's looking. You're fearless." In thirty-three years, I'd never heard him say that. Best compliment he's ever given me. I told him I should tattoo it—fearless.

When I asked what he liked least, he hesitated. Finally, he said,

# The Road That Led to Love

"You drag yourself down too much. You don't believe in yourself the way I do."

He said it wasn't who I am, just something life handed me. That's us in a nutshell. He sees fearlessly when I can't. I pull him into depths he'd rather skip. Oak and wildflower. Frustrating and faithful. Rooted and scattered. Storm and sunshine—still growing together.

The Road That Led to Love

## Changing the Narrative

Some mornings I wake up sad and heavy, like there's a storm cloud hovering over me that no one else can see. I start missing friendships that don't feel like work — the kind where you don't have to chase someone down or beg to be included. It's a pity party in my head, and I'm the guest of honor.

I've learned that there are countless ways to spend time, not just physically, but mentally. Where we let our thoughts linger shapes everything. And sometimes, I catch myself lingering in the wrong places: disappointment, loneliness, resentment. Those thoughts might feel justified, but they don't lead me anywhere good.

Bart and I had just gotten back from a trip. It was mostly wonderful, but it also peeled back some layers we'd been ignoring. The kind of things that quietly pile up until they demand to be dealt with. We love each other, but we both want what we want — and sometimes those wants don't match. That's when the crossroads appear: someone has to bend, or we both decide if the road we're on is still worth it.

The truth is, I can't change Bart. I can only change me; my reactions, my tone, my focus. Yesterday morning, I woke up thinking, I'm done. I felt that familiar spiral start to pull me under. But then I took a breath and thought, What if I change the story in my head?

## Backroads and Backporches

What if instead of replaying everything that's wrong, I remind myself of what's right?

Bart loves me. I love Bart. I'm grateful for what we have.

It's not perfect. It's not even easy most days. But it's ours — messy, real, layered with history and hope. I know what I want in my life, and Bart's always been a part of that picture.

So I changed the narrative.

That doesn't mean I ignore the hard things. It means I refuse to give them the microphone. I redirect the story toward truth and gratitude, not because it fixes everything, but because it keeps my heart soft enough to stay.

As I've always said, "Where your focus goes, so goes your life." My mind can still be a battlefield, but I'm stronger now. Strong enough to pause, breathe, and steer it toward peace. Strong enough to enjoy the small moments that remind me love is still here, even when it's quiet or complicated.

And now and then, I let myself cry, not just for what's happening now, but for the parts of me that still ache, the parts that don't quite know where they belong. When that happens, I don't shame her anymore.

I just give her a break.

What I've learned is that changing the narrative isn't about pretending. It's about choosing to tell the truth with kindness instead of pain. It's realizing that love can be both broken and beautiful at the same time. And it's knowing that peace isn't something you stumble upon — it's something you build, one thought at a time, by turning toward the light instead of the storm.

# The Mental Game

Even after you change the narrative, your mind sometimes circles back — whispering old stories, replaying doubts that you thought were already healed.

This morning was one of those times.

I sat here thinking, God, what in the hell is wrong with me?

I'm on this porch, my favorite place, in a beautiful home, with a husband who loves me and kids who love me. Maybe they don't always know how to show it, but I know they do. They just show it in their own ways.

Still, something is missing.

And that's the part that gets me. What do I need? Am I just exhausted? Tired of trying to get people to want to be with me, to love me, to really see me? Or is it just me, me, me? Am I so damn focused on myself that I can't see anything else?

The mental game gets so old.

I know I'm blessed. I can list my reasons, count them one by one, and still there's this ache that creeps in. The kind that whispers, You should be happier than this. It's the quiet battle no one sees, the one between the life I have and the peace I keep trying to hold onto.

Sometimes I wonder if it's not about what's wrong with me at all — but what's still healing in me. Maybe this isn't selfishness. Maybe it's exhaustion from a lifetime of trying to be okay. Maybe it's the soul asking for a breather — not from love, but from holding it all together.

So I sit here. I breathe. I let the questions stay unanswered for now. Because sometimes, there's nothing to fix, just a heart that needs a little grace while it finds its footing again.

Backroads and Backporches

# When Intimacy Feels Complicated

---

This isn't easy to talk about—but it matters.

When you've lived through trauma, it doesn't just stay in your memories; it settles in your body. Mine has been through it: years of sexual abuse, emotional and physical pain, betrayal, surgeries gone wrong, shutdowns. Scars and echoes. Silence in places that used to speak.

The passion has always been there; my love and desire for Bart are real, but my mind and body don't always cooperate. Sometimes parts of me feel distant. Like I'm there and not fully there. Touch doesn't always register. Intimacy can feel like navigation more than connection. Living in my body is exhausting sometimes, but I keep showing up.

Memories didn't start returning until 2017. For years, I floated above my body during intimacy and assumed it was normal. Disconnected. Out of place. Easier not knowing. Easier to drift than sit with pain. I hate admitting it, but sometimes it felt easier not to know.

There are moments I disconnect, not on purpose, but because my body has learned it. Dissociation protected me once; now it can steal presence from the most tender moments. Sometimes I choose the distance because it feels safer than being present when my body isn't ready yet. Not ideal—just honest.

My husband shows up. He tries. He's steady in his way, and I know I'm loved. Still, intimacy isn't simple for us.

We miss each other sometimes—not for lack of love, but because connection can be complicated. Understanding the way each of our brains works differently has helped us find a rhythm that feels more like us. It wasn't a magic fix, but clarity always helps.

He doesn't always catch subtle cues or know when I need closeness versus space. I can be loud with emotion; he can retreat into logic. Sometimes I'm too much; sometimes he feels like not enough. We speak different emotional languages, but we keep translating. That's the work.

# The Road That Led to Love

Therapy has given us tools to build a connection beyond words, learning to meet each other in mind, body, and spirit. No quick fixes. Slowly, we're finding new ways to reach for each other in places we used to get lost. You're never married too long for therapy. Honestly, most people today could use a wise outside voice to balance this wild modern life.

Once, during an argument, I said, "I feel like I'm disappearing." Bart said, "Then I'll wait until you come back." And he did. That changed me.

We're not perfect. We're still in it. That counts.

"Healing isn't a straight road—it's a gravel path with potholes, thorns, and wildflowers. And sometimes, the person walking beside you trips too. But the miracle? You help each other up." And we keep walking.

## Pull-Starts and Love Tanks

---

This hit me while yanking the cord on our old gas mower. Pulled and pulled—nothing. The tank was bone dry. Marriage can be like that.
Bart's a push start. Flip the switch, ready. Me? I'm a pull start, like a lot of women my age. Menopause is a trip. Cramps, childbirth, hot flashes, mood swings—and now an engine that won't turn over without a little priming.

Here's the thing: you can't roll over at 10 p.m. and expect fireworks if you haven't pulled the cord since breakfast. Connection doesn't start in the bedroom—it starts in the hallway, the kitchen, the "I see you" look across the room. It's a hand on my back while I'm doing dishes, a text that says, "You're doing amazing."

Menopause also hands you a megaphone: "No more people-pleasing. Say what you mean." If you haven't been pulling that cord since 1998, buddy, you might be out of luck.

The good part? When I feel seen, loved, and safe—I rev like a Harley. A loud one.

Moral: Keep pulling. Every day. With heart. With purpose. A full love tank makes for an engine worth revving. And yes—your person needs it, too.

The Road That Led to Love

# Glimmers in the Chaos

Marriage is hard. Life is hard. Love isn't perfection—it's persistence. It's choosing each other again, even when you're so mad you could throw a spatula. (Maybe I have. Once or twice.)

We've had seasons of minimal eye contact. Heavy days. But we've also danced barefoot in the kitchen and had mornings where I looked at him and thought, Thank God we're still in this.

Yesterday Bart finished a new corner in the backyard, "The Spot." It's where I breathe. Incense, maybe a joint, some tea, and the day falls off me. It's not just a place—it's a hug shaped like a backyard.
Out there I thought: I love my life. My husband. My kids. This home.

We forget, in the chaos, that beauty still shows up. The glimmers. The sparkle. The stuff you can't photograph but that fills your soul.
My advice: Don't make the hard the headline. Feel it, say it, handle it—but don't crown it. Love is noticing. Encouraging. Holding onto the good.

Sometimes love folds towels in silence. Sometimes it's sitting side by side, both on your phones, still feeling safe. Sometimes it's catching each other's eyes in the kitchen, knowing you made it through another day without losing your minds.

After a week where everything went sideways, I sat beside Bart and asked, "We good?" He squeezed my hand. "Yeah. We're still us."
Now we name those moments. I'll say, "That was a glimmer." The air shifts. We remember: we're still here. Still choosing.

This life isn't always polished. But it's ours. And the glimmers are everywhere if you're willing to see them.

"Don't let the hard parts convince you the whole thing is broken. Sometimes it's just a storm. Sometimes it's just a Tuesday."

We keep showing up. Keep laughing. Keep breathing each other in—and giving each other space.

Because at the end of the day, that's love.

Choosing each other.

Again. And again. And again.

# Let's Get to the Good Roads

It hasn't all been hard. We have plenty of beautiful roads.

We've road-tripped across the USA, turned the car into a rolling home, and collected memories like postcards. Arizona deserts under skies so wide they made us feel small. Mexico's ocean rhythm drawing us closer. Vermont, New Hampshire, and Maine awash in fall color; Boston's brick streets and old stories. Savannah's cemeteries and crumbling buildings, curious tales lingering in the air. San Francisco's hills, the chill bay wind, the Golden Gate rising from fog—still chasing wonder together. He's my favorite travel partner.

The good roads are at home, too. Morning coffee waiting. A glance that says more than words. Grocery runs that become inside jokes. Evenings on the porch when the sun dips low and everything feels right. He fills my gas tank without being asked. In Buda City Park, I geeked out over mushrooms and Bart, unprompted, filmed me—then asked me to take one of him. We're weird. It works.

Milestones: Thirty-two years ago, two broke kids sat at the Hyatt in downtown Austin with champagne, a marquis diamond, and a dinner we couldn't afford. We slipped out without tipping and laughed nervously down the elevator, praying the waiter wouldn't follow. That was us—broke, nervous, in love, saying yes anyway. I'd say yes all over again.

We've carried that yes through babies and bills, anniversaries and masquerade balls, first pedicures (he loved it), and dating each other even when I don't feel like going, because by the end of the night, the laughter shows up and the spark returns.

When I say he's my person, I don't just mean steady. I mean hubba hubba. After thirty-three years, that's still how I feel about Bart Steele. He's my person, my partner, my hubba hubba. The love is steady, the fire still burns—and yes, I still think he's hot.

The Blue Shirt

Hanging up clothes, a normality of this life
But contemplative.
Contemplative because he is here.
Here? My husband, not physically and not by chance.
Chance is but a moment,
But moments make a lifetime.
Time is what it takes.
Lots of time, lots of memories.
Memories of a blue shirt that smells like him
And memories of good times.
Times like these are meant to be contemplated.

## Ending Thought – The Roads That Didn't Break Us

Some roads should've ended us—and some I'm still not sure about.
We've had fights that felt like final straws. It's getting easier. Therapy, books, and time have helped me keep my head on straight… most days. We've had seasons we barely touched. Arguments over money, parenting, sex, faith, and the grocery list. We've slammed doors. Gone to bed angry. Said things we didn't mean, and swallowed things we should've said.

But sometimes, you get another chance.
Not the pretty, buttoned-up kind of grace. The gritty kind. The kind that says, "You're hard to love right now, and I'm still here." The kind that shows up with coffee, a prayer, and sometimes a gummy after a rough night. The kind that apologizes first. The kind that pulls you into a hug even when you're still mad, and melts the edge.

If your marriage is more backroads than freeway, map crumpled, GPS dead, that doesn't mean you're lost. Some of the best views come after the bumpiest rides.

We're not done. Not even close. I picture a screened-in back porch down the road—Bart's gray hair in the breeze, grandkids or grand-pets underfoot, and I smile, because we kept going until it got easier.
That's the road we're on—together.

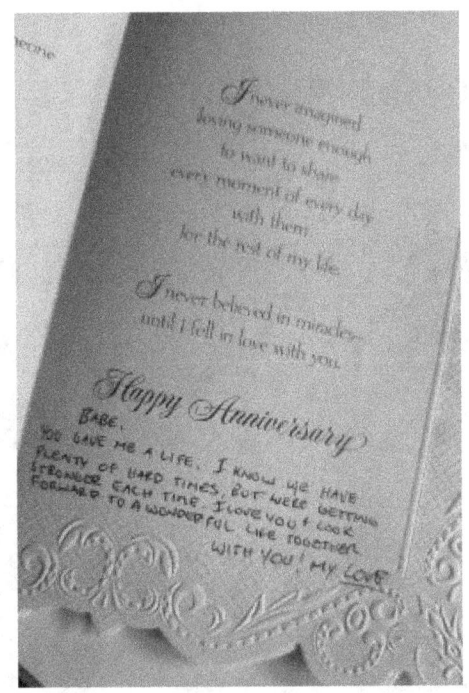

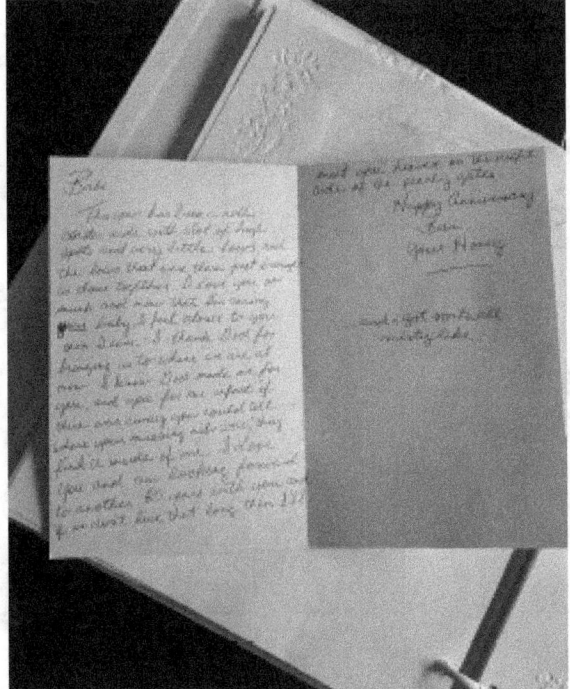

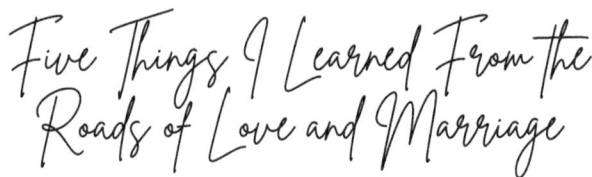
## Five Things I Learned From the Roads of Love and Marriage

**1. Write your story. Revisit yourself.**
Reading our story reminded me why we started, who we were, and how far we've come. When you trace your own roads, you reignite the spark that got you here in the first place.

**2. The hard seasons don't erase the good ones.**
When life gets noisy with bills, babies, and silence, it's easy to forget the laughter. But joy and struggle run side by side. You just have to look for them again.

**3. Grace doesn't always look gentle.**
Sometimes grace shows up messy—through tears, laughter, or a hug you weren't ready to give. Real grace doesn't wait for you to deserve it; it just stays.

**4. Passion doesn't fade—it matures.**
It's not always fireworks anymore. Sometimes it's a soft touch, a shared glance, or laughter that turns into something more. The flame might change color, but it still burns.

**5. The best roads are the ones you keep choosing.**

Love isn't a destination—it's a decision. You wake up, look across the table, and say, "Yep, it's still you." And somehow, that's the most romantic thing of all.

# Part Three: The Roads of Friendship

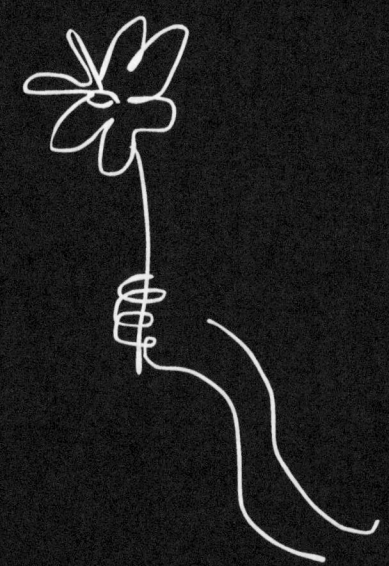

## Wildflowers and a Stranger Named Marcela

On the beauty of unexpected friendship.

It was the spring of 2023, and Texas was showing off.

The wildflowers were wild and crazy that year—fields of color that looked like someone had spilled God's paintbrush across the land. I'd been taking more back-road trips with my camera, chasing that feeling I get out there—free, grounded, wide open.

I posted on Instagram asking if any of my photographer friends wanted to join me for a day of shooting the blooms. A couple said yes, but at the last minute, both canceled. One messaged and said, "Hey, I have a friend who might want to go if you're okay with that."

Her name was Marcela.

I didn't know her from Adam, or Eve, and, to be honest, it felt a little strange agreeing to spend an entire day on the road with a stranger. But something in me said, Why not?

We met in the Sam's Club parking lot. Her boyfriend at the time dropped her off with her camera bag slung over her shoulder. She smiled, climbed into my car, and from the second we started driving, the conversation just flowed.

She was about Breanna's age, early thirties, and had just moved to the States from Mexico. A world traveler, she'd spent years photographing people and places around the globe, leading workshops and creative retreats. I listened, fascinated, thinking how brave that sounded. Then she asked about me. So I told her about how photography became my lifeline, my way of noticing what's still good and beautiful in the world.

# The Roads of Friendship

We spent the whole day talking, laughing, shooting, and getting a little sunburned. Met at eight in the morning, and I didn't drop her off until close to seven that night. By the end of the day, it didn't feel like I'd been with a stranger. It felt like I'd known her forever.

Marcela and I have been friends ever since. She's become like a daughter to me, one of those people who walk into your life and just stay. Watching her plant roots in Austin, finding her voice and rhythm, makes me proud.

That day reminded me of why I love meeting new people. Friendship, for me, has always been about the unexpected—about being open to whoever shows up on the road beside you.

We limit ourselves when we only befriend people who look, think, or believe like we do. Some of my closest friends don't share my views at all—and that's the beauty of it. I've got straight friends, gay friends, atheists, agnostics, Muslims, Buddhists, married, single, Republicans, Democrats, Independents, Libertarians, and a few still figuring it all out.

If I can't be friends with someone who thinks differently than I do, that says more about my fear than my faith in what I believe. If I really believe what I believe, why would someone else's view shake me? And if I'm wrong—well, that's how I'll learn.

Some of the best growth in my life has come from people who see the world nothing like I do. Different ages, backgrounds, and stories have stretched me, challenged me, and reminded me not to live in a bubble. Without those differences, life can get small and a little bitter. But when we keep showing up with open hearts, it stays real—and that's where the beauty is.

There's still so much good in the world, even if it hides behind all the noise. The good people aren't the ones shouting about it. They're the ones quietly out there living it—kind, humble, and too busy doing good to make a scene about it.

And that's the kind of good I want to notice, be part of, and keep alive in my own small way.

"Friendship doesn't always begin where you expect. Sometimes it starts with a DM, a handshake, and a shared tank of gas."

## Backroads and Backporches

# The Messy Beauty of Friendship

Learning to Hold Loosely and Love Deeply.

Friendship has always been both beautiful and hard for me. Once I let someone into my heart, they stay there, even if they walk away. For years, that kind of loyalty felt like both a blessing and a curse. I couldn't understand how people who once felt like family could just drift off or disappear. It used to ache deep, like a bruise I kept bumping into.

But time and life have taught me a few things. I've learned to breathe with it, to understand that relationships have their own rhythm. Some people are meant to walk the whole road with you, and some are just meant to walk a stretch. I don't grip so tightly anymore. I still love deeply, but I've learned to let go more easily.

Before I could really understand friendship, though, I had to learn how to be one to myself. That took some work. I had to ask: Would I want to be friends with me? Do I actually listen? Am I kind, or just polite? Those questions aren't always comfortable, but they've been freeing. My circle keeps getting smaller, but the peace inside it has grown. Maybe that's just life — less noise, more meaning.

Friendship isn't tidy. It's messy and real. It's showing up with puffy eyes and yesterday's mascara, or dropping off a bag of dirt and a plant because your friend knows you need to get your hands in the soil, because 2020's been rough, and you just need something alive to care for. It's those small things that say, I see you. Sometimes it's just sitting there together, passing tissues back and forth while Elmo, my Goldendoodle, tries to comfort us.

The best friendships aren't the ones that always feel easy. They're the ones that have weathered all the crap life throws your way, the ones that still show up with Kleenex, prayer, and a bottle of whiskey. They don't flinch when things get weird or uncomfortable. They don't keep score. They don't need an explanation before love steps back in. Those are rare, and worth hanging onto.

## The Roads of Friendship

Over the years, I've had every kind of friend, the steady ones who've been around since my teens, the ones who burned bright and then drifted off, and the ones who just get me without words.
The steady ones are like porch lights that never go out, even after years, they're still there, ready to welcome me home.

The seasonal ones? They came in like fireworks, bright, bold, unforgettable, and gone before I knew what happened. I used to take that personally. Thought maybe I did something wrong. But I've learned that not every friend is meant to stay forever. Some are here to teach you something or help you through a season. That's not failure. That's just life doing what it does.

And then there are the forever ones, the ones who can read my tone before I finish a sentence. They've seen my walls and love me anyway. We've gotten through a lot with laughter, brownies, day dates, whiskey, and forgiveness. We've said the hard things, rolled our eyes, and still shown up again the next day.

If I let you into my circle, you've got a spot for life — even if we never talk again. When I love people, I love them for good. That doesn't mean I chase. It just means I carry them in memories, in songs, in random moments when something reminds me of them, and I smile instead of ache.

The older I get, the more I realize friendship isn't about constant contact, it's about connection. It's that quiet knowing that you're seen, that you matter, that you belong. It's less about being everyone's cup of tea and more about being your own kind of brew, strong, imperfect, and real.

Because the best friendships aren't polished; they're practiced. They're lived-in, a little dented, full of laughter and forgiveness. They make room for space and silence, and they always find their way back around. At this stage of life, I don't need a crowd. Just a few good people who know when to hand me a shovel, a drink, or a hug — and who don't flinch when I hand one back.

# Can Men and Women Really Be Just Friends?

---

Not every road of friendship is easy to talk about, and this one has been on my mind for a while — can a married woman and a straight man really be friends?

I think they can (I had been told all of my life that was a big no-no)! But it takes awareness, honesty, and a good dose of common sense.

I spend a lot of time around men, photographers, contractors, artists, gallery folks, clients, you name it. Most of the creative and building worlds I'm part of are male-dominated, and friendships happen naturally when you're working side by side, traveling, or sharing ideas. I enjoy those friendships. They bring different perspectives, and I learn a lot from them.

But let's be real, people love to read into things. A laugh, a coffee, a shared story, someone always wants to make it something it's not. And that used to make me shrink back a bit, second-guess myself, like maybe I was doing something wrong just by being friendly. I'm not anymore. I've just learned to stay grounded and pay attention to my own heart.

For me, there's a clear difference between being open-hearted and being careless. I can have a genuine connection without crossing a line. I can value conversation, humor, and trust without it needing to turn into something complicated.

Bart knows who I am and how I am. We talk about things openly, which helps keep everything clear. He's creative too, so he gets it, connection and collaboration are part of what keeps us alive. Still, I know what my priorities are. I know who I go home to and who I share my life with.

The truth is, friendship, no matter who it's with, only works when you're honest about your intentions. You've got to know where your boundaries are and respect theirs, too. You have to be able to say, "This is important, but not worth losing what I already have."

## The Roads of Friendship

Some of the best conversations I've ever had have been with men who saw me as a person, not a project. They challenged my thinking, made me laugh, and never once made it weird. Those friendships remind me that the connection between people, any type of person, is a good thing.

At the end of the day, friendship is friendship. It's about respect, not gender. It's about honesty, not assumption. It's about showing up as yourself and trusting that the people who really know you, including your spouse, know your heart too.

Like every road worth traveling, this one just takes awareness. You've got to keep your eyes on the path and your heart where it belongs. Because connection is a gift, but protecting your peace is, too.

# Backroads and Backporches

## Unexpected Friendships
---

How the right people find you, anyway.
It's funny how the right people find you when you're not even looking. I was in Port Aransas, one of my favorite little towns to disappear into when I need to breathe again. I'd been spending a lot of time there—taking photos, walking the beach, and just letting myself slow down.
There's this small coffee shop I love there, cozy, kind of bohemian, the smell of espresso and sea salt mixing. It's the kind of place where people linger instead of rushing out, where the regulars know each other by name.

That's where I met Emily.
She was the barista—young, grounded, and bright-eyed, the kind of person who has light about her even when she's tired. We started talking one day while she made my drink, just small talk at first. But that day, I told her about this girl I'd met in Austin who'd invited me to a picnic in the middle of a park—blankets, a little cheese board, wine glasses, the whole fancy setup. I laughed and told Emily, "We should bring fancy picnics back!"

Without missing a beat, she said, "Let's go on one tonight after I get off work."

And just like that, we did.

That evening, we spread out a blanket on the beach, pulled out snacks and drinks, and sat under the sky like two old friends who had known each other forever. She was half my age, but it didn't matter—there was this natural connection between us. We talked about everything: life, heartbreak, healing, and the strange ways people find each other right when they need to.

At one point, she told me something I've never forgotten. She said, "I used to walk into a room thinking everybody hated me. Then I decided I could choose what I think—so now I walk in believing everybody loves me."

I sat there staring at her, the waves rolling in behind her, thinking, that might be one of the wisest things I've ever heard.

## The Roads of Friendship

She was right. You can't control how people see you, but you can control how you see yourself—and how you walk into a room.

That one sentence shifted something in me. If you might be wrong either way, why not choose the thought that lifts your head?

We stayed there until the sky turned navy and the beach lights flickered on. It was simple, unplanned, perfect. Two women, one young, one a little older, meeting halfway in the middle of life, trading stories over snacks and sea air.

I think about Emily often. We still talk now and then, and every time I do, I remember that night and the lesson it carried: sometimes the best friendships aren't planned. They don't announce themselves. They just happen, like a sunset you almost missed but turned around in time to see.

## Patti: A Friend for the Soul

The mentor who taught me to breathe. Patti came into my life back in 1997, and from the very beginning, she felt like a big sister and mentor rolled into one. She taught me about creating a home that feels alive and inviting, not picture-perfect.

Her house was full of scarves, knick-knacks, and art layered with stories. It wasn't about being trendy or following rules—it was about love. From her, I learned not to fill my space with what others say is right, but with what feels like me.

But Patti wasn't just about homes, she was about souls. She had this way about her—steady but free-spirited, strong but tender, a woman who built bridges with her words and held space like it was sacred work.

Our friendship was laced with something deep and quiet. Patti's words weren't just encouragements; they were lifelines. She had a gift for sending me exactly what I needed, right when I needed it, as if God Himself whispered, "Send this to Desiree right now."

Some mornings, before the sun rose, my phone would buzz and her message would slice through my chaos like light breaking through storm clouds:

"Heavenly Father, I come before Your throne this morning with a request for my dear friend Desiree. Father, You see the chaos that she is standing in the middle of right now... Holy Spirit, rise up within her and let the floodgates of heaven be open and fill her this day with the peace that only comes from You."

Other times, it was scripture. She once sent me Psalm 116:

## The Roads of Friendship

"I love the LORD because He hears my voice and my prayer for mercy. Because He bends down to listen, I will pray as long as I have breath!" Then she added, "He bends down to listen… this line has stopped me in my thoughts this morning. How does this scripture influence your understanding of God?"

That was Patti, always pressing me into deeper waters.
She dreamed in community. One day, she texted me about something she wanted to call A Gathering of Sojourners. Not a Bible study, not a program—something looser, truer. A circle of people willing to sit in the wilderness together. She wrote:

"Pilgrims through the ages have always understood that the journey has as much to teach us about ourselves and our relationship with God as the destination. Without the one, our experience of the other is impoverished."

That was Patti, always pulling beauty and meaning out of ordinary days.

And because words were never enough, I once tried to capture what she meant to me in a poem:

On the back porch, eclectic and free,
A sacred space for you and me.
From church pews to the open air,
We found our rhythm, met Jesus there.
No hymns, no walls, no judgment near,
Just love and truth, His presence clear.
The scent of earth, the sky's embrace,
A holy peace within this place.
Some may judge; they'll never see,
The beauty in this harmony.
Two women walking their own road,
With Jesus carrying the heaviest load.
He knows us well, our flaws, our ways,
Yet loves us through our wild, raw days.
Thank you, friend, for holding the space,
For helping me find my sacred pace.

Patti passed in December 2024, and the ache of losing her is still raw. But her words, her prayers, and her presence live on. I scroll back through her texts sometimes, and it's like she's still here whispering reminders:

"No worries. I'm here for you. You are so often in my thoughts and prayers. God let our lives' journey intersect many years ago. You've never left my mind. Love you dearly, friend."

Friendship like Patti's doesn't die—it just shifts form.

She'll always be a friend to my soul.

Bart & Desirae,
 The verse of old comes to mind "A friend in need is a friend indeed" – You both have been that for me many times –
Thank you for the help w/ care for Patrick during Hospice Care. It made a huge difference –
 God Bless you – Ro HJ

## Digital Roads and Social Media Souls

Finding connection through a lens.
When I joined Instagram back in 2014, I thought it would just be a place to share photos, my sunsets, road trips, bits of Texas, and the quiet beauty most people pass by. I never imagined it would become a community that stretched across oceans.

    At first, it felt awkward. I wasn't there to chase followers or hashtags; I just wanted to share my heart through images. But slowly, people started finding me. Not the loud kind of people, but the ones who saw what I saw—the stories in the stillness, the light slipping through old windows, the wildflowers growing in forgotten places.
That's how I met Pearl.

    She lives in England, and somehow our photos found each other before we did. She messaged me about a picture I'd taken, a foggy road, quiet and endless, and she said it made her feel peace. That started our friendship. We've never met in person, but we've talked for years about photography, faith, and life. It's funny how someone across the world can end up feeling like an old friend who just lives in another time zone.

    Social media can be noisy, sure—everyone talking, not many listening. But it's also where I sharpened my craft. I learned how to see through other people's eyes, how to tell stories that reach further than my backyard. I learned how to run a business, how to price my art, and how to stand out without selling out. I met photographers who challenged me to grow, and others who reminded me to stay grounded.
Some days, I scroll through my feed and smile at how many people I've never met but genuinely care about. Artists, moms, writers, travelers, all of us connected through this digital thread that somehow feels personal. It's not the same as sitting on a porch with someone, but it's real in its own way.

## The Roads of Friendship

I've had long conversations in comment sections, shared stories through DMs, and even prayed with people I've never stood next to. There's something about seeing a stranger's art, hearing their struggle, and realizing we're all out here just trying to capture the same thing—meaning, connection, beauty, hope.

Do I let everyone in? No. Trust still takes time. I can be a forever friend who doesn't call weekly or post daily. Real ones don't mind. Because at the end of the day, social media, like life, is just another kind of road, and sometimes the people you meet on that road remind you you're not walking it alone.

# Older Women, Younger Me

Learning by listening.

When I was a young mom, some of the richest conversations I ever had were with the older women at church. They were the ones who'd already raised kids, buried dreams, built new ones, and lived long enough to know that life never turns out exactly how you plan—but somehow, it still turns out beautiful.

I used to watch them sitting together after service, sipping coffee from those little Styrofoam cups, talking about everything from casseroles to heartache. When I finally worked up the courage to join them, they welcomed me right in. They didn't talk down to me or make me feel silly for not knowing what I was doing. They just listened. And when they spoke, it wasn't to correct, it was to guide, to share, to remind me that I was doing better than I thought I was.

They made me feel seen at a time in my life when I mostly felt invisible—tired, worn thin, trying to keep babies alive, bills paid, and my sanity somewhere within reach. They didn't care if my hair was in a messy bun or if I showed up late; they just pulled me into their circle and told me stories about when they were exactly where I was.

Those women marked me. They made me want to grow up and be that kind of woman, the one who doesn't just talk, but listens; who makes space for others to exhale; who helps younger women feel seen and safe enough to be honest about where they are.

Now, all these years later, my back porch has become that space. It's not fancy, just a mix of old chairs, candles, and the smell of whatever's blooming in the garden, but it's where people come to talk, cry, laugh, or sit quietly if that's all they can manage. I tell people, "If you show up, there's always room for one more chair."

## The Roads of Friendship

Sometimes it's my kids' friends stopping by after a long day, or a young woman from town who just needs to talk about life and love and how hard it all can be. Other times, it's me sitting across from someone younger, realizing that I don't have all the answers—but I can listen. And sometimes that's enough.

There's something real about women gathering like that—different ages, different stories, all showing up as they are, no performance, no pretending. And I'll be honest, I have a lot of things in my head that I try to live out, but I don't always do it. I write about it in hopes of doing it, and most of the time, I'm just reminding myself of the woman I want to keep becoming.

None of us gets it right all the time. We just keep trying, keep showing up, and keep learning from each other.

That's the woman I want to be now as the older one—the one who makes space for others to belong, who knows when to speak, and when to just pour another cup of coffee and listen. Because listening—that's where the real learning happens.

# A Soul Connection Time Can't Touch

Love that outlasts time.

My door's always been open to my kids' friends. It's just who I am. Over the years, our house has been a revolving door of teenagers, laughing too loudly, raiding the fridge, tracking in mud, and filling the rooms with a kind of energy that makes a home feel alive.

That's how Andrew came into our lives.

He walked in skinny as a rail, grin first, and made himself at home from the start. He called me Mrs. Steele, sometimes Mother Steele or Momma Steele, and once, when I was on lunch duty at their little private school, he jokingly called me the Polish Dictator. (To this day, I'm still not sure if that was about my last name or my bossy tone, but honestly, he wasn't wrong.)

Andrew got me. He knew that my "don't test me" look always came with love. He was quick to laugh, respectful, but mischievous in a way that made you love him more. He had a brightness about him—the kind of kid you just rooted for.

He wasn't my son, but he may as well have been one of mine. He ate at our table, hung out in our living room, and left his presence in all those little ways that stick. You don't realize how much space someone fills until they're gone.

Andrew's gone now, and it still hits me sometimes out of nowhere. I'll be scrolling through my phone, go to text someone whose name starts with "A," and there he is. His name pops up every single time. And even though I know he'll never answer, I can't bring myself to delete it. Keeping it there feels like keeping a piece of him alive. It's my quiet way of saying, You mattered. You still matter.

That kind of thread doesn't break. It runs outside of time—beyond distance, beyond loss. Sometimes, when I open my front door and see one of my kids' friends standing there, I think of Andrew. I think about how much he taught me about showing up, about how a person can make a mark on your life without even trying.

## The Roads of Friendship

He reminds me why I keep the door open, why there's always a spare plate at my table and an extra blanket on the couch. You never know who needs a place to land or who might need a little mothering that day.

Love like that doesn't have an expiration date. It stays. It lingers in laughter you can still hear, in names you can't delete, in stories that keep finding their way into the light.

Andrew was one of those stories, and because of him, I'll never stop opening my door.

## The Hardest Friendship – Marriage

How we keep showing up.
You'd think marriage would make friendship easy. But it's actually the hardest one to hold onto.

Bart and I have known each other for forty-five years, and in that time, we've built, broken, rebuilt, and laughed our way through just about everything two people can. If he's the only one I get to carry through this life, with all the stubbornness, chaos, laughter, and mess that comes with us, I'll still call it a win.

We've seen every version of each other: young and wild, broke and scared, hopeful and exhausted. There've been seasons when we've been so close we could finish each other's sentences, and others when we could barely stand to be in the same room. He can make me laugh until I can't breathe... and he can make me madder than a hornet in about two seconds flat. Sometimes both in the same five minutes.

We're fire and ice, and neither one of us ever wants to be the first to melt. He's practical and opinionated; I'm emotional and a little too outspoken for his comfort. He likes order, I like ideas. He wants to solve things, I want to talk them to death. And yet somehow, we always find our way back to center — not because it's easy, but because it matters.

What keeps us together? Showing up. Protecting the friendship even when the marriage part feels hard. Laughing when we can, forgiving when we should, and remembering that underneath all the noise, there's love — messy, complicated, loyal love.

## The Roads of Friendship

We still date each other. We go for drives with no destination, just backroads, snacks, and a playlist full of old songs. We watch sitcoms together — he laughs big and loud, and even when I'm mad at him, I can't help but laugh too and then everything from the day melts away. Laughter does that. We go to breakfast on Saturdays and talk about everything and nothing. He makes the best sandwiches and cuts up my salad just the way I like it—a small act that says a lot.

Sometimes we end the day sitting on the porch in silence, letting the air clear. Other nights, one of us will reach for the other and say something like, "You still mad?" and before you know it, we're laughing again.

There are moments of tenderness that sneak up on us, like the time we ended up dancing in the kitchen, barefoot and breathless, no music playing, just the sound of our laughter filling the room. That's the friendship part. That's what keeps pulling us back when everything else feels too hard.

It takes buckets of grace, a lot of space, and more patience than either of us were born with. We've been through enough to know that love isn't always soft, sometimes it's a fight to stay on the same side. But somehow, we do.

Would I choose him again as my closest friend?

Yes. Even when he's driving me crazy. Even when I'm threatening to run away with the dog.

Yes. Every single time or at least today.

"Would I choose him again as my closest friend? Yes. Every time."

# Choosing Your Words.

Because silence is better than poison.
I was sitting at a table full of good women one night—food, laughter, stories, the kind of easy talk that fills you up. Then someone mentioned another woman who wasn't there, and the air shifted. The laughter thinned, and I thought, Damn, I really thought I was going to like this group. I didn't love what was said, but I didn't write her off either. She's actually precious—just a little spicy—and some people process out loud. I get it. I do the same. Let's be honest, I'm an over-sharer. Thus, this book.

What I've learned is that gossip rarely introduces itself as gossip. It usually sneaks in dressed as concern or just venting. But poison is still poison, even if it's poured into a pretty glass. Words have weight, and once they're out, they hang there. You can't unsay them. I can't control what other people talk about, but I can control what I add to the room. It's not my job to manage anyone else's voice, it's my job to mind my own.

So these days, I choose quiet more often. If I can't say something kind, I let it pass. I'd rather be known for laughter than whispers, for encouragement over noise. And honestly, silence isn't weakness, it's wisdom. For some of us, learning to hold it takes a whole lot of damn work, but the peace that comes with it? Totally worth it.

# The Words That Anchored Me

What I say to myself on dark days.
I once asked a friend to describe me in three words. They didn't hesitate.

"Brave. Lovable. Loving."
At the time, I didn't realize how much I needed to hear those words, or how much they'd stick. But they did. They found their way into the cracks of my heart and settled there like anchors.

Now, on the days when my mind turns against me, when I start replaying old mistakes or believing lies about who I am, I whisper those words to myself. I am brave. I am lovable. I am loving.
Some days it feels like I'm saying them just to keep my head above water. Other days, I believe them with everything in me. Either way, I say them—because the words we repeat become the truths we live by.

Brave isn't about never being afraid—it's about standing up again after you've fallen a hundred times. It's showing up when your hands are shaking and your heart's tired. It's doing the next right thing, even when you don't know where it leads.

Lovable isn't about being perfect or easy to be around. It's about knowing that you deserve love even when you feel unworthy of it. It's remembering that being loved doesn't require earning it—it just means letting yourself receive it.

And loving… loving is the one that gets me every time. Because love is a choice. It's a verb. It's what I keep trying to do even when I'm hurt, disappointed, or worn out. Loving is how I remind myself that I still have something to give.

I used to think kindness was soft—that it meant being a pushover. But I've learned that kindness is power. It's what builds bridges, heals wounds, and quiets storms inside you and around you. It's not weakness—it's strength under control.

## Backroads and Backporches

So on the dark days, when the noise in my head gets too loud, I come back to those three words. I write them in my journal. I breathe them in. I let them replace the old voices that used to tell me I wasn't enough.

Because I am brave.
I am lovable.
I am loving.
And that's enough.

Photo Credit: Michael Tarabay

The Roads of Friendship

# What Friendship Means to Me Now

Growing wider, not smaller.
Not everyone will get you. That's something it's taken me a lifetime to learn. But if even one person truly sees you and doesn't flinch, that's enough.

I've spent years trying to figure out where I fit, only to realize I'm not meant to fit neatly anywhere. I'm a wildflower. I don't grow in rows. I sprout where I shouldn't—stubborn, bright, sometimes overlooked, always me. Some people walk right by. The right ones stop. Those are my friends.

For most of my life, I tried to hold onto everyone, to make sure every relationship stayed tidy and intact. But friendship doesn't always work like that. People change. Life shifts. Kids grow up. Jobs move you. And that's okay. I've learned to let people come and go.
If you stay, I'm grateful. If you don't, I'm still okay. New people always show up right on time, and the ones who are meant to stay, stay without being chased.

A while back, Breanna told me I should write a chapter about friendship. She said, "Mom, you've maintained so many friendships over the years, and your ability to create community is one of your strongest qualities."

That one sentence stopped me in my tracks. I hadn't really thought of it like that before. To me, friendship has always just been part of life, natural, necessary, the way I breathe. But she's right. I've built connections that span decades, cities, and seasons, and even when people fade in and out, the roots remain.

## Backroads and Backporches

Breanna's words made me think about what friendship really means at this stage of my life. It's not about how many people are around me anymore, it's about the quality of the connections I keep. It's about having people who can sit with you in the dark and celebrate with you in the light, without needing you to be one or the other.

Lately, our little town has surprised me. I've met new people who push me to grow, as a person, a friend, and a businesswoman. Joining the Chamber opened a door to community I didn't know I needed. I've found people who cheer me on, who show up, who make me laugh when I'm taking life too seriously. They remind me that no matter how old we get, there's always room for new friendships.

Life isn't meant to be lived in a bubble or balanced entirely on our kids' shoulders. They'll fly—and they should. But we still need people. It's on us to build friendships, pour into others, and stay open to connection across generations.

Every season teaches something new if you're open to it. Some lessons come through laughter, some through loss, and some through the simple joy of sitting on a back porch with someone who just gets you.

I used to think my friendships were all over the map, but now I see they're just part of one long, winding road—different paths, same heart. And honestly, I wouldn't want it any other way.

Photo Credit: Michael Tarabay

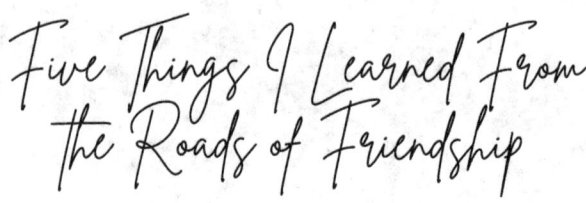
# Five Things I Learned From the Roads of Friendship

**1. Not every friend is meant for every mile.**
 Some people are with you for a season, some for a lifetime. Letting go doesn't mean it wasn't real, it just means you've both reached a different exit.

**2. The best friendships feel like breathing.**
 You don't have to perform or shrink. You can be quiet or loud, broken or blooming, and still be loved in the same measure.

**3. Honest friends don't just nod—they nudge.**
 They call you out when you're off course and clap when you find your footing again. Real friendship has both truth and tenderness.

**4. New people don't erase the old ones.**
 Your heart has room to grow in every direction. Each person adds something, laughter, wisdom, perspective, and the road keeps widening.

**5. Being a good friend sometimes means giving space.**
 Love doesn't always look like showing up; sometimes it looks like stepping back so someone else can breathe.

*Maybe friendship isn't about who walks beside you the longest, but who makes the walk feel lighter while they're there.*

The roads of friendship taught me how to connect.
The next ones would teach me how to find peace in my own company.

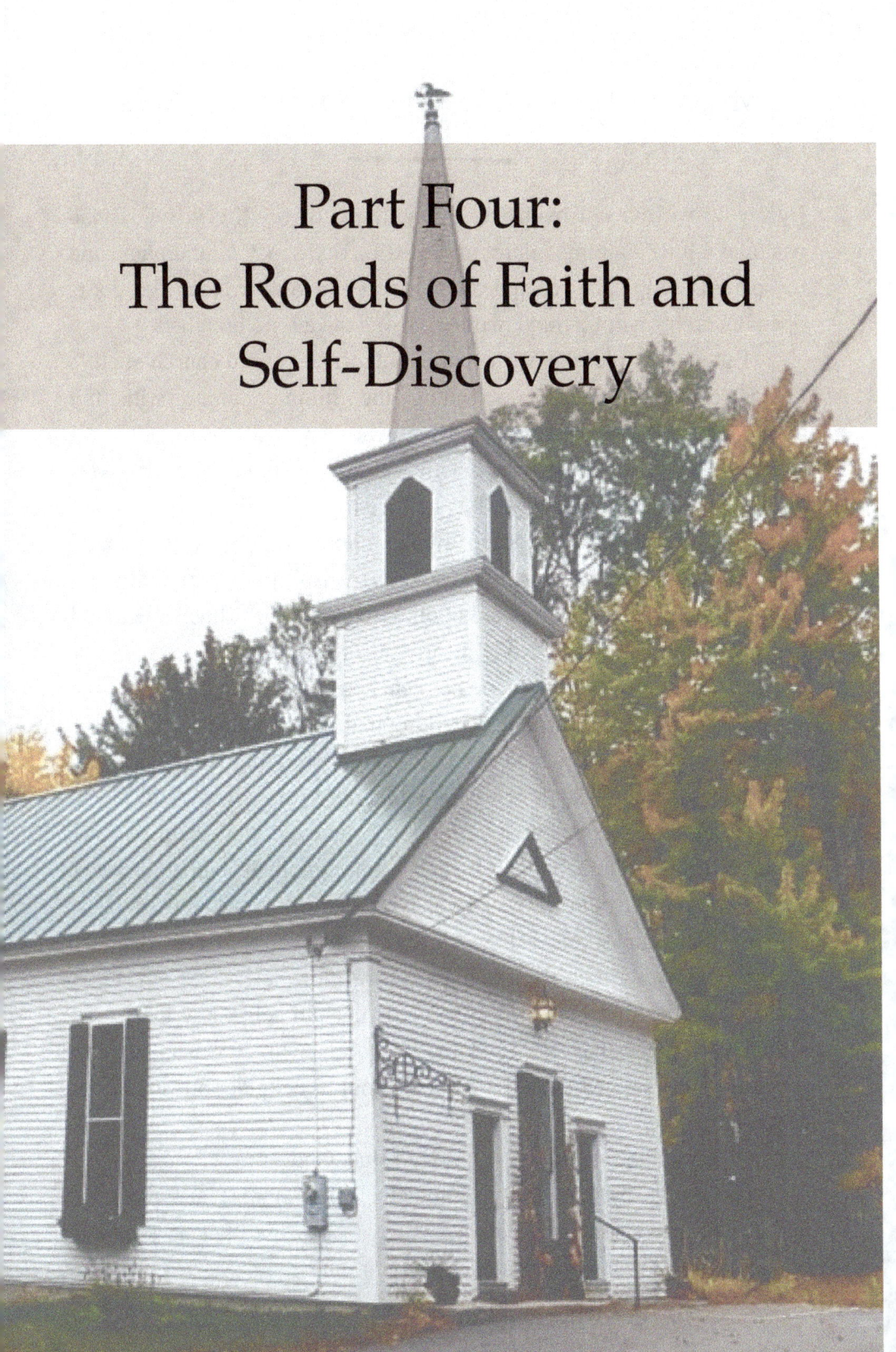

# Part Four:
# The Roads of Faith and Self-Discovery

# My Faith Didn't Die—It Outgrew the Walls

I grew up with God woven into every thread of my life. My Grandad pastored a little A-frame church in Del Rio, Texas. My Grandmama and my parents sang, played, and did whatever it took to keep the doors open. Church wasn't a Sunday thing; it was the air we breathed.

But the summer that truly marked me wasn't about church at all. I was eleven or twelve, spending the summer alone with my grandparents. It was the first time I saw who they really were, not just a preacher and an organ player, but two ordinary, stubborn, courageous people who quietly lived what they believed.

One afternoon in that small living room, I watched my Grandad marry a Black man and a White woman. It wasn't illegal anymore, but in the South, it was still frowned upon. Grandad didn't flinch. He stood there, Bible open, hands steady, heart sure. I didn't have to ask why. I saw it in his face—the same love he preached about every Sunday.

In that moment, I learned something that would shape my life: love mattered more than rules, and compassion mattered more than opinion. That moment planted something in me that no sermon ever could.

And yet, even with the church surrounding me every day, the moment I remember most didn't happen in that little church. It happened years earlier in Alaska, when I was five, lying in the grass with my doll Christie. The air smelled like pine and woodsmoke, and the sky stretched so wide it felt like it could swallow me whole.

Alaska was the first place my little five-year-old self knew there was something bigger than me. Out there in the open, it was quiet and peaceful—just sky, wind, and a feeling I couldn't explain but somehow understood.

Not church-God. Not preacher-God. Just God.

Those two moments, my Grandad's quiet courage and that day under the Alaskan sky, rooted something deep in me that no scandal, hypocrisy, or church politics could ever tear out.

## Faith Isn't a Straight Line

If mine were a road map, it'd be full of curves, wrong turns, gravel detours, and a few stretches where I ran out of gas on the side of the road. Sometimes it's been a Sunday drive with the windows down, music up, wind in my hair. Other times, it's been me parked on the shoulder, trying to catch my breath and figure out which direction I'm even supposed to be facing.

But here's the truth: my faith never really left me.

It just outgrew the pot it was planted in.

I've lost count of how many times I've heard, "Desiree, you just need to stay where you're planted."

Clearly, those people don't garden.

Only plants that stay in the same pot forever quit growing—and I've never been good at staying in one place for long anyway. Roots need space. Soil needs renewal. Sometimes the pot has to crack wide open before the plant can breathe again.

That was me, rootbound, tired, gasping for room to grow.

I don't remember a time when I didn't know about Jesus. His name was as familiar to me as my own—sung in hymns, echoed in Grandad's sermons, whispered in Grandmama's quiet prayers. But when I was nine, something shifted. I didn't just know about Him—I knew Him.

At nine, I made a choice. I wanted Jesus in my life, though, truth be told, He'd been there all along.

Up to that point, I had already been hurt by people who should have protected me, adults who crossed lines that should never be crossed. I didn't have the words for it at the time, but I knew it was wrong. I felt dirty. I felt afraid. I felt small.

And then one day, something inside me rose. The air in the room was heavy, thick with dread, as it always was when he came near. My body knew the pattern: freeze, wait, endure. But not that day. That day, something changed.

I became brave enough to pull his hand away.
It wasn't loud or dramatic. I didn't scream or shout. It was quiet but firm—the kind of quiet that says, This ends here.

I looked him in the eye, and everything in me said, No more.
And from that day forward, I stayed away from him until he died.
That courage wasn't mine alone. I knew it. I felt it.

It was Jesus—steady, present, alive. Not the distant Sunday-morning version, but the One who shows up in the middle of the mess and whispers when you can't even speak: You are Mine. You don't have to take this anymore.

And I believed Him. I never let that hand touch me again.
For years, that was the only memory I carried—the one my mind allowed me to keep. I could feel the shadows of more, but my brain did what brains do when the pain is too much: it locked the rest away, threw away the key, and probably left a note that said, "Do not disturb." I prayed to never remember. And for a long time, I didn't.
But at fifty-two, the lock finally broke open. The memories came, one by one, and I had to see the rest of the story. It was brutal. It shook me. But now I can say—I'm better for it. Because remembering is what started the real work of healing.

And healing, I've learned, isn't a finish line. It's a long, uneven road, sometimes you limp, sometimes you crawl, but you keep moving. I don't even know if healed is the right word for something like this. But I do know this: I'm still walking. And I'm still here.

That moment at nine was the first time I knew Jesus was real—the first time I felt Him rise up in me. And even when my own mind tried to protect me from the truth, He stayed. Steady. Patient.

Waiting for the day I was strong enough to face it

# Betrayal at Fourteen

By fourteen, I was still showing up to church every chance I could, but most of the time, I was doing it alone. My parents had stopped going, but I still wanted to be there. It was the one place I thought I could belong.

Until the night that changed everything.

It wasn't a rebellion. It wasn't wild teenage behavior. It was one night at my house—a handful of us kids being goofy and curious. Someone found a bottle of whiskey, and we each stuck a finger in, tasted it, and laughed. That was it. A silly, harmless moment that should have faded by the next day.

But it didn't. Word got back to the pastor, and before long, everyone knew.

He called a special meeting for all the young people and their parents. My parents didn't go to church, so I showed up alone. I remember sitting in the very back pew, heart pounding, trying to act invisible.

He didn't say my name, but he didn't need to. He said everything but my name, and everyone knew exactly who he was talking about. I could feel the air shift as he spoke, like the oxygen had been pulled out of the room. Every word landed heavily. I could feel eyes on me—even if some of them never turned my way.

When it ended, I slipped out, found a quiet spot outside, and sat in the grass, shaking. An older girl came and wrapped an arm around me and let me cry. When I finally stopped, I went home … alone.

The silence in that house was deafening. No one was there to ask what happened or how I was. That night, the shame was crushing. It was the first time I wanted to end it, and the first time I tried.

No one called the next day. No one knocked.

And yet, beneath the noise, a whisper: You are Mine. You don't have to take this anymore. I didn't understand it then, but looking back, that whisper was proof I wasn't alone.

# Numbing the Ache

After that night, I didn't go back for a long time. The place that once felt safe now stung like salt on a wound. So I did what a lot of hurting teenagers do — I found a way to quiet the noise: alcohol.

At first, it felt like an escape. Then it became a habit. Eventually, it turned into survival. People saw the loud laugh, the party girl, the one who looked like she didn't have a care in the world. What they didn't see was the ache underneath, the girl crying in bathroom stalls or staring at the ceiling, wondering if life would ever feel worth it.

I drank to forget, and most of the time it worked — until it didn't.

That night, I left a bar angry at a guy I'd been seeing. He had taken another girl home, and I remember storming out, keys in hand, fueled by pride and pain and too much to drink. I took a wrong turn onto a dark road. Later, I'd find out he saw me leave and something in him said, Follow her.

He did.

He watched my taillights disappear, then saw them flip, once, twice, three times, before the truck landed crumpled in a ditch. He ran to me, pulled me out, and called my dad on one of those giant cell phones straight out of 1992.

When my dad got the call in the middle of the night with "sir, your daughter," he expected the worst. The next day, he went to the wrecking yard to see the truck. The man working there met him at the gate and said, "Sir, I'm so sorry. The person driving that truck couldn't have made it."

My dad said, "She did. That was my daughter, and she's fine."

The man just stared and said, "I've never seen anyone walk away from a wreck that bad."

That's when I knew there was something more to this life. I didn't know what that reason was yet, but I knew I'd been given another chance.

That wreck became the turn that led me straight into Bart's life — and, eventually, back toward faith again.

## From Survival to Second Try

After years of running, I wanted something solid under my feet. I was tired of the hangovers, the heartbreaks, and the noise in my own head. I craved steady ground.

Bart was that for me.

When we found our way back to each other, I didn't come with a halo; I came with a list. Before we ever said "I do," I looked him straight in the eye and said, "If you don't quit smoking pot and go to church with me, I won't marry you."

He quit.

He went.

Things changed… later.

And at the time, that felt like victory. I thought faith wrapped in a building was safety, if I could just get everything in order, maybe the chaos inside me would finally quiet down.

For a while, it worked. It was beautiful in its own way, Sunday mornings, community, purpose. We were young, trying hard to build something that looked like a good life. I learned to cook a little better, laugh a little louder, and show up when people needed help. We made friends who became like family, and the rhythm of church life gave me structure.

But underneath it all, there was still me, a wildflower planted in a row of neatly trimmed hedges. And the truth is, not everyone knew what to do with that.

There was a certain way women were expected to look, talk, and behave. I tried for a while to fit the mold: the long skirts, the no-makeup Sundays, the quiet smiles even when I wanted to scream. But pretending gets heavy, and my soul was starting to suffocate.

## Backroads and Backporches

By twenty-seven, I'd had enough. I walked into my pastor's office one day, heart pounding but clear-headed, and said, "I've studied this out. I've read the Bible, the book on standards (the one that wasn't technically required reading but might as well have been), and even a book by a woman who left the UPC and challenged that mindset. I don't believe wearing pants, cutting my hair, or wearing makeup are sins. I won't be a hypocrite in front of my kids. I wear them everywhere else, and I'll wear them to church, too."

He looked at me, probably expecting an argument, but all he said was, "Okay, Desiree."

That was it. And honestly, what was he supposed to say? No one was going to change my mind. I knew what I knew.

I remember thinking, That's all? After all these years of rules and judgment, just okay?

But that was all.
I walked out lighter than I'd walked in. It didn't make me fit better, but it made me free.

That was the first time I stood in front of spiritual authority and said, I know who I am, and I won't pretend to be anything else.

I don't know if it was me walking into that office that changed things, but not long after, every woman in that church was finally free to wear what she wanted. And suddenly, I was getting a lot of, "Desiree, you are so brave…"

To this day, I still laugh at that. I never understood why wearing pants to church made me brave.

I was just tired of wearing pantyhose!
Looking back, I'm still proud of that young woman — the one who didn't know she was starting a quiet revolution, just by being honest.

It wasn't a rebellion. It was freedom.

And for me, it was the beginning of learning that faith doesn't grow in control — it grows in authenticity.

The Roads of Faith and Self-Discovery

# 2017–2020: The Unraveling

Life kept moving, and for a long time, it looked good from the outside: marriage, kids, church, work, and all the pieces that are supposed to mean you've "made it." I played my part. I smiled in pictures, showed up when I was supposed to, and said the right things. But cracks don't always start where people can see them.

Faith, marriage, motherhood, they all have seasons, and mine were starting to shift. It wasn't loud or sudden; it was a slow, quiet undoing. There's a kind of exhaustion that doesn't live in your body—it lives in your soul. I had everything that was supposed to make a woman happy, yet something in me was unraveling. I kept pushing through, because that's what I do. Keep the house running, love the kids, hold the marriage together, hold me together. But underneath the routine was a steady hum of grief I didn't yet understand.

People say 2020 was the year the world stopped. For me, the slowing began three years earlier.

In 2017, when Grandmama died, the ground shifted. She wasn't just my grandmother—she was the one who felt like home. Her kitchen smelled like cornbread and garden tomatoes, and her hugs felt like safety. When she left, something in me broke loose. The silence she left behind gave space for something else to rise, the memories I had buried so deep I thought they were gone for good.

One of my abusers came back to me in flashes I couldn't control. It felt like my mind had been holding a box closed for decades, and finally decided, She can handle it now.

I wasn't ready. But ready or not, there it was.

I prayed for the box to close again, but it didn't. And in hindsight, I'm glad it didn't—because even though remembering broke me open, it also began the work of freeing me.

Then came the next hit: skin cancer. Another crack in the pot. My body was telling the truth, my mouth still couldn't. It was like everything I'd been holding in for years was forcing its way to the surface, grief, fear, anger, truth, all of it demanding to be seen.

## Backroads and Backporches

By 2020, the cracks were everywhere. The world was coming to a stop, but I had already been forced to slow down.

That year, I went in for what was supposed to be a simple breast reduction. It didn't go as planned. A surgical mistake nearly cost me my life. I came out of it scarred in ways no mirror could show. My body was weak, stitched up, and in pain—but my heart hurt worse.

I remember sitting on my back porch, bandaged inside and out, staring at the trees and trying to make sense of it all. The air felt heavy, like the world itself was sighing. Everything was unraveling: my body, my beliefs, my sense of control, and I couldn't stop it.

Church, the place that once claimed to have all the answers, had started to slip out of focus long before then. I'd sit in services and listen to sermons that no longer fit what I knew deep in my bones. I couldn't reconcile forgiveness that kept abusers in power while survivors were told to stay quiet. I couldn't find God in the rules, but I could still find Him in the wind that brushed across my porch.

Did I lose faith?

No. Not in Jesus. Never in Him.

But I did lose faith in the institution.

And as strange as it sounds, that loss became a beginning. It was the start of something real. The start of freedom.

I didn't know it yet, but the same wildflower that once stood up in that pastor's office was still there—weathered, battered, but alive. And through every loss and every crack, she was learning something new about herself: that even when the soil shifts and the roots feel exposed, growth can still happen.

That's the thing about wildflowers. They don't need perfect conditions to bloom.

They just need a little light and the will to keep reaching.

---

By the time 2020 rolled around, I was exhausted — body, mind, and spirit. I had survived so much, but I didn't even recognize who I

## The Roads of Faith and Self-Discovery

was anymore. My days felt heavy, and my faith, the one thing that had always anchored me, suddenly felt too small for all I was feeling.

I remember sitting on my porch one evening, wrapped in a blanket, notebook in my lap, watching the sky change colors. The world was quiet in that strange 2020 way: no plans, no people, no distractions. Just me and my thoughts.

For the first time in years, I let the real questions surface. Not the ones that fit neatly into a sermon, but the kind that rattle around in your chest until you finally say them out loud.

"God," I whispered, "how in the world can every single soul, from the beginning of time to the end, believe exactly like I do? How can billions of people from every culture, every background, all see the same thing and still find You?"

I had been raised to believe that we were the ones who had it right. But life had introduced me to too many good people who didn't look, think, or worship like me, and they believed just as deeply.

I still believed what I believed. That hasn't changed. But I also knew the God who made every color of sky and every language on earth couldn't possibly fit into one human explanation.

As the breeze moved through the trees, I felt an answer settle somewhere deep inside:

They can't. But I can answer all their questions.

Simple. Clear.

And I laughed, partly out of relief, partly because it was so obvious. I'd been trying to fit an infinite God into a human-sized box, like pouring the ocean into a Mason jar.

That moment didn't make me lose faith; it made me love it again. It was the beginning of a wider kind of belief, one that left room for mystery, for difference, for the possibility that God meets each of us where we are.

That night, I stopped needing to be right and started wanting to be real. And that shift, that quiet, porch-light revelation, was the first step toward the freedom I'd been craving all along.

## What Broke Me

It was watching abusers keep their power while survivors were told to stay quiet.

It was realizing that church folks could quote Scripture but couldn't sit with someone who was hurting.

It was hearing forgiveness used like a muzzle.

It was sending something deeply personal to pastors, a piece of my story, a plea for understanding, and hearing nothing in return.

Not one response. Silence. And silence, I learned, is a response.
That's when it hit me: the ones I trusted to carry my story weren't safe. The walls I thought would shelter me were echo chambers.

But Jesus never ghosted me. He didn't turn His head. He didn't go quiet when I dared to be honest.

I found Him on my porch, steady in the wind, humming through the trees, present in the stillness. The porch became my meeting place, my breathing room, my truth-telling space. I stopped trying to pray the "right" way and just started talking to Him like I would a friend.

Faith, I realized, isn't about everyone believing the same. It's about showing up as you are and trusting that God can handle every question, every doubt, every heart that's searching.

That moment on the porch didn't fix everything, but it rewired something deep in me. It was the day I stopped trying to shrink God to fit my understanding and finally let Him be as big as He's always been.

# A Poem for the Porch

I am usually alone,
I talk to myself.
I go where I want to go.
I cry. I laugh. I dance. I sing.
And I breathe.
No one sees—
But He does.
The porch is my pew,
The wind is my choir,
And my heart, my cracked, scarred,
healing heart,
Is the only altar He ever asked for.

# A Call to the Little Church

If you carry His name, don't confuse silence with care. People heal in presence, not absence.

If you lead, lead like Jesus, toward the margins and into the mess.

Stop using forgiveness to keep people quiet. Boundaries are part of love.

Make space for questions. God isn't threatened by curiosity.

Fund care, not just buildings.

Bless the wildflowers—some of us bloom best on backroads.

# The Stranger Who Saved Me

It was one of those days when the world just felt too heavy.

I was parked in my camper by the beach, crying so hard I could barely breathe. I'd been carrying too much for too long—pain, memories, the constant trying and pretending. I remember whispering, I just can't do this anymore.

I wasn't praying, journaling, or reaching out. I just wanted the sound of the waves to drown out the noise in my head.

Then my phone rang.

I almost ignored it. Unknown number. The last thing I wanted was conversation. But for some reason, I swiped the screen anyway.

"Hello," I said—short, sharp, still catching my breath.

A man's voice came through the line. "Hello! How are you today?"

"NOT GOOD," I blurted out, louder than I meant.

He paused, clearly surprised, then said gently, "I'm sorry to hear that. May I ask what's wrong?"

I didn't answer. I figured he was some telemarketer running through a script. He went back to his pitch, then stopped mid-sentence.

"I need to circle back to what you said," he told me quietly. "You said you're not good."

Something in the way he said it cracked me open. There was no sales voice, no script—just concern. Genuine, human concern from someone halfway across the world who didn't know me but cared anyway.

## The Roads of Faith and Self-Discovery

We talked for almost two hours. He didn't try to fix me or preach. He just listened. He let me cry. He asked gentle questions that showed he was really hearing me. His voice stayed calm and kind—steady, patient, present.

When we finally hung up, I wasn't magically okay. But I wasn't alone anymore either.

I sat there for a long time, staring at the ocean, waves rolling in like deep breaths I hadn't been able to take all day.

A Christian woman, crying in her camper on the Texas coast, and a Muslim man in Pakistan had just shared one of the most honest conversations of my life.

A Muslim saved a Christian that day.

I still call the Spirit that moved in that moment Jesus. Maybe he calls it something else. But I know it was the same love—the same heartbeat that threads through all of us, no matter where we live or what we believe.

That call didn't change the way I see God; it deepened my faith in how big He really is—and how beautifully intertwined we all are.

Because love isn't limited by religion, geography, or language.

When it shows up, you recognize it.

And that day, love showed up in the voice of a stranger.

# The Bars Around My Heart

In a meditation class once, the instructor said, "Open the window of your heart."

My first thought: Well, hell no. My window has bars.

And it did. That's how I'd lived most of my life—bars up, love out, nothing fully in. It felt safer that way. I could love hard and deep, but never let anyone love me back all the way. Control disguised as protection.

Then came yoga—and yoga, bless it, sneaks up on you.

People probably think I've gone full wilderness here, but stay with me: I've found more of my faith on a yoga mat than I ever did in a pew.

There's something about being upside down in silence that makes you honest. When you're standing on your head, you can't hear the world's noise, or everyone's opinions, or even your own to-do list. It's just you, your breath, and God trying to keep you from face-planting.

# The Roads of Faith and Self-Discovery

You process the junk life hands you on a yoga mat in ways you never see coming. I've ugly-cried in downward dog, found forgiveness in child's pose, and had full-on conversations with Jesus in savasana. I'm convinced He rolls His eyes at me sometimes—but He's there, keeping pace with my breathing.

I don't do yoga to "empty" my mind; I do it to fill it back up with what matters.

Faith isn't about a building anymore; it's about that quiet space where my soul, my mind, and my body finally agree to show up together.

Maybe that's not typical of Christian faith, but that's fine by me.

Jesus is my guide, my balance, my strength—even when I'm wobbling or falling out of a pose. Connecting with Him doesn't require kneeling at an altar; sometimes it happens when I'm trying not to topple over in tree pose.

And the beauty of it all is that no one can tell me differently, because I know what I know—and it's my own damn road.

Even there, in resistance, I sense Him. Not scolding or shaming—just steady.

I can almost hear Him saying, I know. I'll stay here until you're ready.

That's the God I trust now—not a warden, not a checklist, not a sermon.

A companion patient enough to sit with me—or stand on His head with me—until the hinges on my heart finally loosen.

## My Wildflower Faith

I've never been an oak tree—steady, rooted deep in one spot. I've always been a wildflower.

Wildflowers don't stay where they're planted. Their seeds blow with the wind and bloom where they land.

Some call that restless; I call it resilient.

For years, church people told me to "stay planted." But I knew if I did, I'd wither.

I wasn't made to be trimmed into shape or confined to someone else's pot.

I was made to grow wild, stretching toward the sun, bending in storms, finding beauty in unlikely places.

That's my faith now, a wildflower kind of faith.

Not neat, not contained, but free, strong, and alive.

Sometimes I bloom in cracked soil, sometimes on backroads where no one notices.

But I'm still here, still growing, still wild enough to believe that God delights in me as I am.

Because He made me this way.

And here's what I've learned: all our roads look different.

Even Bart and I, after decades of walking side by side, raising kids, building a life, and sharing a faith—still see things through our own windows.

We can stand in the same moment, doing the same thing, and yet be living two completely different stories.

And that's okay. That's how it's supposed to be.

## The Roads of Faith and Self-Discovery

Life's too big to think everyone should see it the same way.

Faith is too personal to fit into one mold.

The road is too winding to pretend we all walk it the same.

I've stopped worrying about how other people are living, loving, hating, or figuring it all out.

Does that mean I don't care? Sort of, at least not the way I used to.

Because honestly, what can I do about it?

Everyone's got their own road to walk, their own lessons to learn, their own God-moments waiting to meet them when they're ready.

I finally understand that I can love people without trying to fix them.

I can pray for them without needing to change them.

I can let them be—just as I hope to be allowed to be myself.

My faith has grown roots and wings at the same time, rooted in what I know, open to what I don't.

It's not about who's right or who's wrong anymore.

It's about walking my road honestly, loving as I go, and trusting that the same Creator who shaped the mountains and the oceans also shaped me, and everyone else, on purpose.

These days, I care less about being understood and more about understanding.

Less about convincing and more about connecting.

I figure if I keep my heart soft, my sense of humor intact, and my porch light on, God can handle the rest.

So I'll keep blooming where the wind carries me, wild, free, and grounded in grace, knowing I don't have to understand everyone's road to respect that they're on it.

That's the beauty of a wildflower faith: it doesn't need permission to grow…it just does.

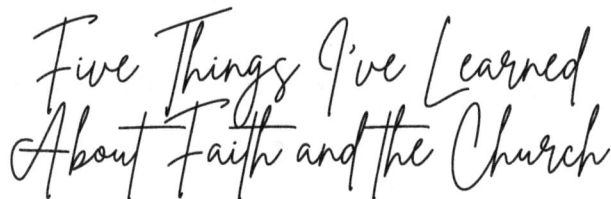

# Five Things I've Learned About Faith and the Church

**1. God never lived in the building — He was always on the porch.**
I finally stopped confining Him there.

**2. The loudest voices aren't always the most loving.**
Real love sits with you and doesn't need a microphone.

**3. You can lose your religion and still keep your faith.**
When the pretending died, faith started to breathe.

**4. Grace doesn't always look graceful.**
Sometimes it's survival, messy tears, and trying again.

**5. I was made to be a wildflower in a world of manicured lawns.**
Faith can be free and still be true.

*In the end, I didn't give up on faith; I just quit trying to squeeze it into places it no longer fit. I escaped what was never real and found what always was: a God who meets me right here on my porch, no makeup, no pretending.*

*I still believe in the little church, the ones who love quietly, who pray without needing to be seen, who show up with casseroles and real conversation. I still want to sit with all the older church ladies and glean from their wisdom, soak in their stories, and laugh about potluck mishaps.*

*I still believe in hope, even when I have to pick it up again and again. And I still believe in a God big enough for every question, every doubt, every wild detour.*

*So if you're reading this, wondering if you've gone too far or fallen too hard, hear me — you haven't. You're still breathing, still becoming. And as long as you've got a little porch light left in you, there's still time to bloom.*

*The porch didn't mark the end of the road; it was just a rest stop.*
*Faith taught me how to breathe again, but life would soon teach me how to stand back up.*
*The same cracks that once broke me became the places where light started to slip through.*
*And that's where the next part of my story begins.*

## The Journey That Unfolded Along Backroads and Backporches

---

As I mentioned at the beginning of this book, my love for photography started in my grandparents' living room. I can still picture myself sitting cross-legged on their carpet, flipping through stacks of National Geographic magazines, traveling to far-off places without ever leaving their couch.

That's where it began for me — learning that photographs could tell stories, stir emotions, and hold onto something fleeting.

By the time I was seventeen, right before I graduated from high school, that spark had turned into something much deeper. I became obsessed with Ansel Adams — his black-and-white landscapes, his use of light and shadow, the way he made the earth itself feel alive. His photos didn't just show places; they told stories. I wanted to do that too. I remember one day in particular. I was having a really hard time, the kind of day where everything feels uncertain and heavy. I decided to drive out to Lake Travis with my little Kodak camera. I had splurged on a roll of black-and-white film, which at the time felt like a big deal.

I wasn't doing anything serious with photography back then — it was just for fun — but that day, sitting there by the lake, something changed in me. I can still feel it, even now as I write this, the way the light shifted across the water as the sun began to sink, the trees glowing from behind, the soft ripples turning silver.

I remember just sitting there, watching, breathing, completely still. And as I sat there, I knew. I didn't know what it would turn into, but I knew photography would always be a part of me.

Back then, I was looking into art schools to study photography. But we were poor, and that kind of dream wasn't in the plans for us. You don't go to art school to become an artist. You get a job, pay the bills, and tuck those dreams away for later. So, that's what I did.

## The Roads Where the Light Shifted

When I graduated, I went straight into the workforce. I never went to college, though I guess my eighteen years of homeschooling taught me how to figure things out on my own. I've always been one to teach myself whatever I needed to know. And maybe that's what prepared me for the creative life I live now — one built from curiosity, persistence, and a whole lot of faith and determination.

About twenty years ago, that old passion resurfaced and became something much deeper. My sister had a stroke, and the photos I'd taken of her helped bring her memories back. That moment changed everything. It showed me that photography isn't just about beauty — it's about preservation. It's about love, history, and legacy.

That realization eventually grew into the brand Backroads & Backporches. It began as a way to slow down and notice, to capture the stories that matter before they fade away. But it became so much more than a business — it became a calling.

Photography has been my lifeline through some of the hardest seasons of my life. When everything felt heavy, I turned to nature. Through my lens, I found peace. Standing on a quiet coastline, pausing on a winding backroad, or simply watching sunlight spill through the trees reminded me that beauty still exists — even when life hurts. Especially then.

We live in a world that moves so fast. Buildings vanish. Trees fall. Landscapes change. People come and go. Without photographs, those stories disappear. That's why I don't just photograph people — I capture places, textures, and moments that are here today but may not be tomorrow.

Over the years, I've been blessed to share that work in Austin galleries and beyond. In 2024, I was honored as a featured artist at the Texas Photography Festival. I also spent a year documenting the behind-the-scenes of an award-winning documentary on equestrian therapy — an experience that showed me how art, resilience, and healing all find each other when you slow down long enough to see.

That's what Backroads & Backporches is really about — noticing. It's about traveling when you can, sitting still when you must, and surrounding yourself with beauty that reminds you to keep moving forward.

Each photograph I take carries a piece of that message. Whether it hangs on a gallery wall or in someone's living room, I hope it invites people to pause — to see the extraordinary hidden inside the ordinary.

# Five Things I've Learned From Photography

**1. Art really can start anywhere.**

Mine started in the middle of my grandparents' living room floor, flipping through old National Geographic magazines. I didn't know it then, but those pages were shaping how I saw the world — teaching me that you don't have to travel far to find wonder. Sometimes it's right in front of you; you just have to be still long enough to notice it.

**2. Light always finds a way through.**

Some of my best work has come from the hardest moments. When life felt heavy, I picked up my camera and went outside — and without fail, the light would shift. That moment — when you catch light breaking through darkness — is the same feeling I get when peace finally settles in my chest after a storm. That's what keeps me shooting.

**3. You don't need permission to create.**

No one handed me a degree or a manual. I learned from curiosity, trial, YouTube, and a whole lot of grace. I still mess up shots, still learn something new every day. But that's part of it — art grows right alongside you. You don't wait until you're ready; you start where you are and figure it out as you go.

**4. Every photo is proof that love existed.**

A photo freezes something that time is trying to erase — a glance, a laugh, a place that once held life. That's why I take so many pictures of my family, of backroads, of ordinary things. Because someday, they won't look the same. And I want to remember how it felt, not just how it looked.

**5. The extraordinary hides inside the ordinary.**

 I've found that if you slow down — like really slow down — you'll see it everywhere. Morning light through the trees. Rust on an old truck. A porch swing waiting for company. The world preaches "hustle," but photography keeps whispering, "Be still." And in that stillness, I find beauty every single time.

*Photography has never just been about taking pretty pictures for me. It's how I breathe. It's how I process life and make sense of all the noise inside me. It's my way of talking to God — of saying, I see You here.*
*Every time I step behind the lens, I remember that beauty still exists — even when life hurts. Especially then.*
*That's what Backroads & Backporches is all about.*
 *Noticing what's real.*
 *Honoring what's here.*
 *And finding light in the places we least expect it.*

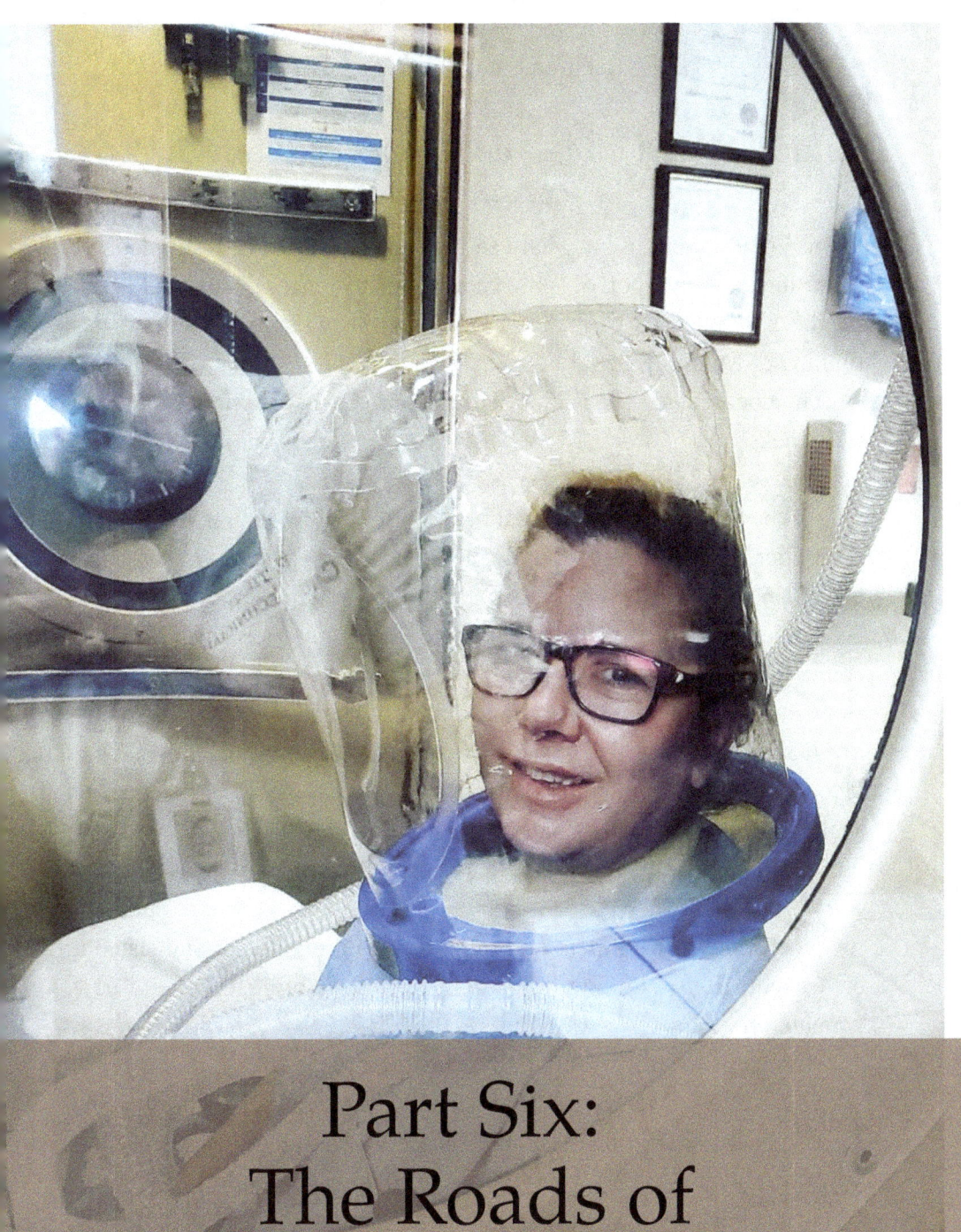

# Part Six: The Roads of Resilience

## Life? It's Just Life — and Sometimes, Life Sucks.

It was 2019. I went in for what I thought was going to be a simple little procedure, a tiny spot of skin cancer on my cheek. Maybe a laser, maybe a stitch or two. Instead, I walked out with forty-five stitches running down my face and lip.

The doctor said, "You'll hardly notice it, and don't move or talk for two weeks!"

Ha! Yeah... okay, Doc.

Maybe he wouldn't notice. But I did. I looked in the mirror and saw a stranger — a woman with a swollen face, stitches snaking across her cheek, and a crooked half-smile that didn't belong to me.

I tried to be grateful. The cancer was gone. But grief doesn't always come wrapped in tragedy; sometimes it comes when your reflection stops looking like you. My smile had always been the one thing I really loved about myself. Losing it felt like losing a part of my identity.
It took time, and a little filler and lip blushing, to get it back. Not the same, but close. Stronger, somehow.

Then came 2020, the year everything fell apart in more ways than one.

I was tired of back pain and migraines, and my doctor suggested a breast reduction. "Nothing dramatic," he said. "You'll feel like a new woman."

He wasn't wrong, just not in the way I expected.

The surgery itself went fine, or so I thought. But within days, something looked wrong. The skin started to darken, the edges turning gray, then black. I called, I texted, I showed up in tears.

He just kept saying, Let your body do what it's supposed to do.

He said it at two weeks, again at four, and again at six, right up until the day he retired and handed me off to his partner.

By then, both nipples were dying, black, hard, and cold. But here's the cruel part: I couldn't even feel it. My nerves had been cut. There was no pain, just the sick realization of watching my own body rot and not being able to stop it.

That's when the real nightmare began.

Wound-care hell: five days a week, two-hour hyperbaric oxygen treatments, then hours of packing and cleaning open wounds that I couldn't feel, just see.

I went to St. David's in South Austin — the Wound Healing and Hyperbaric Center. The first time they rolled me back, I thought it might be like one of those spa pods I'd seen online. Nope. Not even close.

It was a long, hospital-grade chamber, steel and glass, white and sterile, pressurized like an airplane underwater. Multiple people could be in there at once, each on a stretcher, with a nurse inside the chamber and a technician outside "driving the ship."

They sealed the door with a deep, metallic thunk, and suddenly you were locked in this pressurized bubble, watching the nurse's mask puff slightly as the air thickened. The hiss of oxygen filled the space. My ears popped, my head throbbed, and everything felt heavy, like the air itself was sitting on me.

Inside, we couldn't talk much; voices sounded warped and distant. I remember watching the nurse's eyes, calm, steady, moving from patient to patient, checking vitals, giving a thumbs-up. The technician's voice came through an intercom, directing the process from the other side of the glass.

I always wondered what would happen if something went wrong in there. How fast could they open that door? But I tried not to think about it too much.

Two hours at a time. Five days a week. For ten weeks straight. Sometimes I prayed. Sometimes I stared at the ceiling, following the reflection of the fluorescent lights across the curved glass. Sometimes I just leave my body altogether — drifted into that weird numb place where nothing hurts, but nothing feels good either.

Everyone said, "You're so strong," but I didn't feel strong. I felt gone — physically, mentally, spiritually. I was trapped in a body that looked like a battlefield, inside a machine meant to save what was left.

## Backroads and Backporches

By 2022, after reconstruction, I knew I would never look normal again.

But I was alive.

Inside, not so much.

My nervous system was shot, my confidence gutted, my mind spinning with panic attacks that came out of nowhere, chest tightening, vision tunneling, like my body still didn't trust peace.

So when my therapist, calm, clinical, unshakable, handed me a Ziploc bag one day with a brownie inside, I just stared at him.
He said, "Next time you have a panic attack, try this."

I blinked. "You're kidding, right?"

He wasn't.

I looked at that brownie like it was a felony.

I'd tried marijuana in my early twenties and hated it. It made me feel floaty and disconnected, like I was watching myself from across the room. I swore I'd never touch it again.

But panic attacks will make you eat your words — literally.

The next one hit me at church. Do they really need all those lights and blasting music?

By the second song, my chest was locking up.

We left mid-song, and Bart took me home to calm and rest.

I dug through the fridge, found that brownie, and said out loud, "Well, here we go, Jesus."

One bite. Waited. Nothing.

Thirty minutes later — still nothing.

So I took another bite.

Yeah... should've stopped at one.

Ten minutes after that, the munchies hit, the tears stopped, and I wasn't thrashing or gasping anymore. I was calm. Maybe a little too calm, but damn, it stopped the chaos.

When Bart came home, I hadn't told him yet. I was worried about what he'd think. The kids were there, and I remember wondering what they'd say about their mom sitting there half-baked on a Sunday.
But you know what? I was peaceful. No panic. No fear. Just me,

## The Roads of Resilience

breathing, finally. I told Bart later. He laughed, gave me that quiet, whatever-helps look.

The next morning, I sat the kids down on the back porch and said, "Hey, I'm going to start using marijuana. It helps."

They said, "Awesome, Mom. That's great."

And that was that. That's how I became a stoner.

For the girl who once swore she'd never marry the man she loved if he didn't quit smoking weed, I'd come full circle, sitting there literally eating crow. Or, well... weed.

It's okay — I've got a prescription now, courtesy of the great state of Texas.

Turns out, the thing I was most afraid of became the thing that helped me the most.

It didn't erase the pain; it just gave me space to face it — without falling apart, or ending it all.

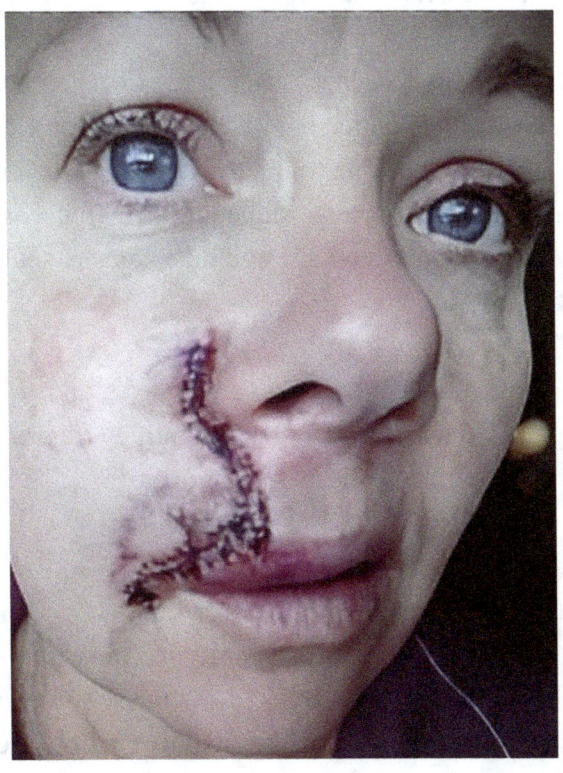

## When the Memories Came

After the surgeries and wound care finally ended, the panic attacks didn't. They still came out of nowhere, chest clamped, vision blurred, heart racing like it was trying to outrun something only I could feel.

My therapist suggested EMDR.

"Sometimes your body remembers before your mind does," she warned.

I laughed. "There's nothing left to remember."

I was wrong.

The first memory had surfaced back in 2017 when my Grandmama Turnell died, but I didn't understand it then. I'd been flipping through an old scrapbook while packing to move into our house in Buda when a flash of something sharp and sickening hit me, another family member's hands, a room, a feeling I couldn't name. I shut the book and shoved it down deep.

But EMDR cracked the lock.

It started slow, a flicker here, a scene there, and then it was like floodgates opening. I'd carried one haunting fragment about my grandpa for years, buried so deep I convinced myself it wasn't real. I told myself I'd imagined it. That I'd dreamed it.

But I hadn't.

Once that door opened, everything poured out.

For two years, the memories came in waves, vivid, detailed, unstoppable. Each one left me wrecked for days, sometimes weeks. It was like living through an earthquake in slow motion. I could feel the tremors long before the collapse.

## The Roads of Resilience

By early 2025, I thought I'd survived the worst of it. I'd faced nearly every ghost my mind had hidden from me. Then came the last one — the Sunday-school teacher.

That memory arrived like a lightning strike. It wasn't just an image; it was sensory. I could smell his house, the wood, the musky smell, and the fried food. I could feel the still air, hear the hum of the refrigerator, and see the sunlight cutting through the blinds like stripes on the wall. And suddenly, I understood why I'd been his "favorite."

Every new memory felt like drowning and coming up for air at the same time. I'd cry until my ribs hurt, shake until my teeth chattered, then sit outside and stare at the sky because there were no words left. Just breath and wind and the sound of birds doing what birds do, reminding me that life still moved.

Healing isn't tidy. It doesn't come wrapped in forgiveness or tied with a bow of faith. It comes with shaking hands, sleepless nights, and the slow, stubborn work of learning to tell that little girl inside me, You're safe now.

Somewhere between those sessions and the sleepless nights, I realized my body wasn't betraying me; she was finally telling the truth I'd been too afraid to speak.

That changed everything.

My body, carved, stitched, scarred, and swollen, wasn't my enemy. She was my witness. She'd carried every secret, every scream, and still hadn't given up on me.

So when Bart looked at me one day, eyes on my chest, and asked, "So what are you going to do about those?"

I smiled. "I'm gonna get a big-ass tattoo."

And I did.

Fierce. Beautiful. Mine.

When the tattoo healed, I looked in the mirror and whispered, Thank you.

Not to the artist. Not even to God — though I know He was there.

To my body.

For surviving every damn thing I put her through.

*Loss has a way of echoing through every season of your life. That wasn't the first time I'd watched everything fall apart.*

## Back in 2008, We Lost It All

Loss has a way of echoing through every season of your life.

That wasn't the first time I'd watched everything fall apart.

Our dream home sat on three acres of Texas soil, wildflowers blooming in every direction, big skies stretching above us. We had a porch we dreamed about, a kitchen we never argued over because, for once, we were in sync. We designed every inch together, wrote scriptures on every post before the sheetrock went up. It was perfect. Ours.

In the spring evenings, the kids would chase fireflies while Bart and I sat barefoot on that porch, talking about forever. That house wasn't just walls and beams; it was the proof that we had built something solid after years of scraping by.

Then the recession came, bold and uninvited, and in what felt like one hard gust of wind, everything we'd built blew away.

I packed the kids' rooms, folded their blankets like I was tucking away memories, walked the halls touching the walls as if I could take a piece of it with me. That house held our laughter, our arguments, our whispered promises that we'd be okay.

But we weren't. Not yet.

We were broke, like food-bank broke. I stood in line holding grocery bags and holding back tears. Humbling doesn't even come close. I remember staring at the canned goods in my hands, thinking how fragile everything really is, how quickly abundance can vanish, and pride doesn't fill a pantry.

Eventually, we found a rental in Austin. No fancy finishes. Loud linoleum that squeaked under your feet. A sad little porch that definitely needed a makeover. The kind of place you don't take pictures of for Christmas cards.

## Backroads and Backporches

But something happened there we didn't expect: we came back to life. We laughed in that kitchen, belly-laughed. We danced barefoot in the living room to bad country songs. We threw parties where millionaires sat on folding chairs and ate off paper plates. I stopped waiting for perfect and just opened the door, and that door opened something in me.

The smaller the space, the bigger the joy. The more we let go of proving ourselves, the more laughter fills the gaps where shame used to live.

There were special dinners, superhero movie marathons, cheap wine, and real conversations that went on too long and ended with somebody laughing till they cried.

Our porch became a gathering place, a little United Nations of faith, doubt, politics, and personality. People of faith, people with no faith, gay friends, straight friends, conservatives, liberals, sometimes all of them out there together. It wasn't messy. It was wonderful, fun, and flat-out beautiful. Nobody tried to fix anybody. We just lived.

That house taught me that community and relationships aren't built by perfection. It's built on openness.

When I look back now, I can see it clearly: 2008 was preparing us for what was coming next. We didn't know it then, but that loss taught us how to bend instead of break. It stripped us of the illusion of control so that when the next storm hit, we'd know how to stand in it.
That house didn't smell fancy—just real—and somehow, that smell felt like hope.

We stopped pretending. We stopped chasing. We stopped waiting for "normal."

And in that little rental, I found something better than normal: peace.

We lost everything we thought mattered.

And somehow, in the middle of all that loss, we found what actually did.

Everything I'd lost, the house, the illusion of control, my sense of safety in my own skin, had stripped me down to nothing but truth. I

# The Roads of Resilience

was raw, restless, and ready for something new.

Time to Move!

And we did.

Looking back now, I can see that the house was just the first layer of loss. Back then, it was our security that crumbled. Years later, it was me. My body. My beliefs. My sense of safety.

But loss has this strange way of circling back, asking you to face what you thought you'd already survived. What I learned through both was the same lesson written in two different languages: you can rebuild from ruin, but you can't rebuild without truth.

That little rental taught me how to live without walls; the healing that came later taught me how to live without armor.
Both roads, through the house we lost and the body that broke, brought me to the same sacred place: surrender.

Because peace doesn't come from having everything together.

It comes from finally letting go.

## How Yoga, Fear, and Stubbornness Collided

As a kid, I was fearless. Climbing trees barefoot, riding my bike down steep hills with no brakes, saying whatever popped into my head before I learned about "tact." I didn't think twice. I just moved — fast, wild, and free.

And then, somewhere along the way, fear moved in. Quiet at first, then loud enough to drown out everything else.

I parented out of fear. Lived out of fear. Smiled through pain and kept my mouth shut out of fear, with most people, anyway. I held everything in, my voice, my needs, my body's warning signs, because fear said if I spoke up, I'd be rejected or labeled "too much." Spoiler: I probably was. But maybe that's because my definition of love came with fine print.

But that's not where the story ends.
After all the surgeries, trauma, and therapy that cracked me wide open, something inside whispered, Move... or you're not going to make it.

At first, it was small, just stretching at home, trying to remember what peace even felt like. My body had become a stranger, stitched and scarred, and I was trying to make friends again.

Yoga wasn't some grand plan; it was a lifeline. I rolled out my mat on the living room floor and followed YouTube videos like I was trying to pass a pop quiz. Some days, I cried through it. Some days I just lie there breathing, trying not to overthink.

And I'll admit, I'd been taught yoga was kind of... questionable. Like if you started breathing too deeply, you might accidentally summon a demon or a drum circle. But here's the truth I've learned: if something brings you calm and doesn't hurt anyone, it's probably fine.

So, I dropped the guilt and kept showing up. Somewhere between the stretches and the stillness, I found something that felt a lot like peace — and I liked it.

## The Roads of Resilience

I practiced alone for a year, just me, my mat, and sometimes Elmo curled up beside me like a furry little sensei. My body started to change, but the real change was in my head. I started feeling grounded again, less like I was surviving and more like I was living.

Eventually, I worked up the nerve to join a yoga studio. I walked in nervously, clutching my mat like a shield, still half broken but trying anyway. The room smelled like lavender and courage. People were breathing in unison, which was weirdly soothing.

That place stretched me, literally and emotionally. I laughed, I wobbled, I fell over, and I cried. It wasn't just exercise; it was therapy disguised as movement.

Then one day, I saw it on the schedule: Ashtanga Yoga.
Oh, fantastic. The Navy SEAL version of stretching.
I'd heard of it, the intense, ego-crushing, "find your soul through sweat" kind. Naturally, I signed up. Because apparently, I enjoy pain and good stories.

The night before class, I made the mistake of watching a YouTube preview. A chipper instructor looked straight into the camera and said, "Ashtanga is the most intense, soul-revealing, ego-shattering form of yoga there is."

Great. I hadn't even started, and I was already emotionally sore.
The next morning, I stood in the bathroom staring at my yoga pants like they were chain-mail armor. I could hear fear whispering, Don't go. You'll look stupid. You'll fail.

And for a second, I almost believed it.
But then I remembered everything I'd already survived: trauma, postpartum, financial collapse, surgery, life itself. If I could handle all that, surely I could handle an hour of organized stretching.

So, I went.

The room was warm and quiet, filled with the sound of synchronized breathing and a faint whiff of essential oils that smelled like commitment. I rolled out my mat and told myself, Just don't pass out.
Halfway through, I wanted to crawl out the door. My thighs were shaking like a newborn calf. At one point, I'm pretty sure my soul

clocked out early and went to sit in the parking lot scrolling through Instagram.

But then came savasana, that final resting pose. Lying there on the mat, heart racing, sweat dripping into my ear, I felt something I hadn't felt in a long time: proud. I whispered, "I did it."

Fear didn't win that day.

And the kicker? I did a headstand, my first one.

I came down laughing, dizzy, half in disbelief, but something in me shifted. The world looked calmer upside down.

From that moment, I was hooked. I started what I now call my headstand journey. Every day, I practiced, against the wall, in the middle of the room, sometimes outside with the wind in my hair and the neighbors pretending not to stare. It wasn't about showing off. It was about quieting my brain long enough to feel peace.

Because when I'm upside down, everything goes quiet. The noise, the worry, the constant buzzing in my head, gone. Just breathe and balance. Standing on my head taught me something that nothing else ever did: sometimes you have to flip your world upside down to finally see it right-side up.

And I swear, somewhere up there, God's watching me, shaking His head like, "That's one way to pray, I guess."

Now, when I walk into class, I don't care who's watching. I'm not trying to be the best. I just want to be there.

And that little barefoot, tree-climbing girl I used to be? She's still with me. Every time I lift my legs and trust my body to hold me, I feel her — wild, brave, unapologetic.

Fear still shows up sometimes, but I've learned how to breathe through it.

I'm not just learning poses. I'm learning me.

The wildflower version.

The one that bends, stretches, and keeps blooming — even after the storm.

And if that's not strength in mind, body, and spirit. I don't know what is.

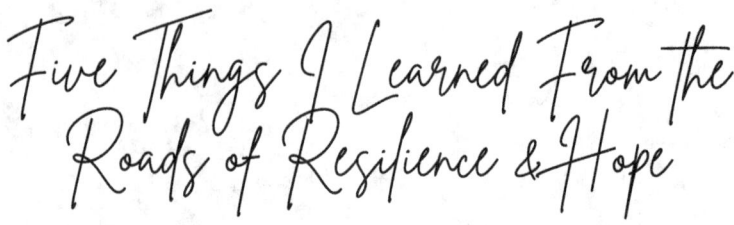

# Five Things I Learned From the Roads of Resilience & Hope

**1 My body wasn't the battlefield—it was the survivor.**
She carried every secret, every surgery, every scar, and still kept me alive. I used to see damage; now I see devotion. She didn't betray me; she protected me until I was ready to remember.

**2. You can rebuild from ruin, but not without truth.**
Losing our dream home, our comfort, and our "someday" plans stripped us bare, but it also set us free. When the pretending stopped, the laughter came back. Truth built what perfection never could.

**3. Stillness is something you practice, not something that happens.**
Therapy, THC, yoga, headstands, and a whole lot of breathing, none of it erased pain, but it gave me space to face it. Calm isn't a place you go; it's something you learn to hold.

**4. Movement heals what sitting still can't.**
Asheville, Terlingua, Port Aransas: the mountains, the desert, the sea. Every mile reminded me that healing isn't about running away. It's about remembering who you are while you move through it.

**5. Joy doesn't wait for perfect—it grows in the cracks.**
Barefoot dancing, porch sunsets, bad country songs, good laughter, joy showed up once I stopped waiting for things to get easier. It was there the whole time, hiding in the ordinary.

# Part Seven:
# The Backroads That Brought Me Home

When I found stillness on the mat, I thought that was it, that healing had finally come full circle. But peace has a funny way of testing itself.

At some point, you've got to get up off the mat, step out the door, and see if what you learned holds up in the wild.

For me, that meant getting back on the road.
The same whisper that once said move now said go. Not to escape, but to explore what healing looked like in motion.

I'd spent years holding my breath.
It was time to breathe new air.

# The Backroads That Brought Me Home

## Asheville: The Quiet That Heard Me

My first solo trip was to Asheville, North Carolina. I'd traveled plenty of family trips, girls' weekends, the kind where you plan for everyone but yourself—but never just me.

Booking that flight was therapy. Renting the car? Victory #2.

At the rental counter, the guy skipped right over me, twice.

Finally, I leaned in: "Hey, dude, I'm down here."

He blinked, then laughed when he realized I barely cleared the counter. I had to step onto the little stool to hand over my license.

Short people problems: legally adult, visually questionable.

That first night, I checked into a creaky 1800s house, floors that talked, walls that sighed, and an attic with Opinions.

In the mornings, I walked misty trails to graveyards and tiny shops, let the fog wrap around me like a hug, and whispered gratitude for simply being there.

I drank coffee in mountain cafés, browsed used bookstores, and learned silence isn't scary when you finally like your own company.

I loved being by myself.

I didn't have to fill every quiet space with noise. It was okay to just be. Bart joined me for the second leg, and we wandered the Blue Ridge, mesmerized at every overlook, stopping for every waterfall.

Beauty is better when your person sees it, too.

# Terlingua: The Soul-Wrenching Adventure

If Asheville was quiet, Terlingua was a reckoning.
I hadn't planned it. I was on the couch, crying the kind of cry that steals your breath. Another memory had surfaced—uninvited, unstoppable.

I whispered, "God, I don't know what to do."

The answer came soft and steady: Go to Terlingua.

"Terlingua? Why?"

Because that's where you were happiest.

By dawn, I'd tossed clothes in a bag, loaded Elmo, and hit the road at 5 a.m.

Eight hours of Taylor Swift's folklore later, I knew the words and felt my chest loosen. Pro tip: never let your tank drop below half a tank anywhere in West Texas. I coasted into town on faith, fumes and literally blowing my car down the highway. Okay, maybe it was just breathing heavily so I didn't have a panic attack.

By sunset, the desert had turned to liquid gold. I stepped out, felt dust under my feet, and remembered why I was there. This was my happiest place on earth!

Nothing is quieter, or more special to me, than West Texas. The silence isn't empty; it hums. The wind carries stories. The stars feel ancient, like they remember you.

My little Airstream sat tucked between the Chisos and the Christmas Mountains, forty-five minutes from anything you'd call a town. Just me, Elmo, and a sky that didn't end.

That night, I stepped out to photograph the Milky Way—millions of stars, the kind of black that hands you back your courage.

Then Elmo growled.

When your dog growls in the desert at midnight, you don't ask follow-up questions.

I bolted inside, locked the door, and became a grown woman hiding

## The Backroads That Brought Me Home

under covers like a five-year-old.

I wasn't scared of people. I was scared of the nightlife: coyotes, javelinas, bobcats, mountain lions… bears if they got the memo.

That night, I grew my bravery.

The desert doesn't flatter you; it confronts you.

It strips you to the truth.

The wind doesn't care what you're afraid of.

The stars don't judge your mess.

They just keep shining until you remember.

You're small, but never forgotten.

I hiked. I wrote. I took photos.

I sat in a silence so deep it felt like prayer.

And somewhere between the stillness and the stars, peace slid into my bones and made itself at home.

# Port Aransas / South Padre: The Road Home

Then came the coast—my favorite rhythm. It started four summers ago as an experiment: a few weeks away to clear my head.

Now I go two to four weeks every year, mostly alone.

At first, those trips were heavy. Some days, I cried the whole walk back from the water. Some days I wrote for hours and left pieces of those pages right here in this book.

Some days, I just laughed and played in the surf like a kid.

This past July, something shifted.

For the first time in forever, I was just… okay.

No tears. No breakdowns. Just breathing. Just being.

Every morning, I sat outside the camper with my coffee, watched the sun climb over the dunes, listened to seagulls argue like it was their full-time job.

I whispered, You're okay.

And I was.

Not all beach moments are Zen.

One afternoon, a woman strolled up: "Are you here by yourself?"

"Yeah, just me."

Then her husband appeared.

"Oh, you're married? Your husband let you come here alone?"

I blinked. "I'm fifty-two. I don't need permission to go to the beach."

They were… recruiting.

I laughed, wished them well, and removed myself from their extracurriculars.

People don't know what to do with a woman who travels alone.

That summer, something else came back: my dance.

A friend and I wandered into her favorite beach bar, flip-flops counted

## The Backroads That Brought Me Home

as dress shoes, and the floor was half sand, half dirt. The band kicked in, and before I knew it, I was moving.

Not for anyone. Not to look cute or hide pain.

Just because it felt good.

Live music wakes me up from the inside out.

When the beat hits, my body remembers joy before my brain does.

Barefoot under string lights, I laughed and danced like I was shaking hands with the girl I used to be, the one who loved life with her whole damn heart.

She's back.

The ocean. The road. The rhythm.

They've all been my teachers.

Every backroad, every porch, every stretch of sand carried me closer to peace.

The world looks calmer now, not because it changed, but because I did.

Healing didn't arrive with a parade.

It came in pieces: road trips, headstands, long drives with no destination, nights that turned into barefoot dancing on the sand.

When I think of the places that have held me—the mountains, the desert, the sea, I realize they were all leading me home.

Not to a house.

Not to a person.

Home to me.

That's where Backroads and Backporches was born, on the road, wind in my hair, nobody else's voice in my head.

Just me, learning to breathe, to love myself and to be good company for my own soul.

If you can't be okay with yourself when you're by yourself, *how can anybody else be okay with you?*

That's what the road taught me.

That's what the porch reminded me of.

And that's where I finally found peace.

The road taught me how to breathe again.

The porch taught me how to rest.

Somewhere between the long highways, the quiet mornings, and the salty wind, I realized I wasn't chasing healing anymore; I was living it. Coming home wasn't about returning to a place.

*It was about returning to myself.*

The woman who once packed her bags to find peace, is now unpacking it—one ordinary morning at a time—right where she is.

## The Woman Who Came Home

This morning, I stepped onto my back porch with coffee and said, "Good morning, world."

I've always loved mornings—quiet, full of promise. But after 2017, mornings came heavy, crowded with thoughts that didn't have names yet. Some days, I woke up tired in my soul.

Over time, I learned to work with it.

To let hard mornings be hard and still find my way back.

That's why I started talking to the morning again—whispering Good morning even when it didn't feel like one. Sometimes saying it out loud brings it back.

On good mornings, I stretch and ease into the light.

On hard ones, I reach for what I call my "anointing oil," THC oil. It slows my brain just enough to sort the noise instead of drowning in it. If the noise keeps shouting, I hit the vape.

Some people won't get it. That's okay. I'm not auditioning.

Maybe I am a stoner. I'm also alive.

So, I thank God for weed and keep breathing.

The air is cool, the sky is waking up, and I remember:

I'm still here. Still choosing to stay.

I used to think coming home meant arriving—safe and familiar.

Now I know it's remembering who you are after you forgot for a while.

Home isn't a house.

It's that quiet unclench in your chest when you stop fighting your own reflection.

I still have hard days—the bars around my heart rattle, and I pull back before I know why.

Now I catch it. I pause. I breathe.

I remind myself: I don't have to be right to be at peace.

## Backroads and Backporches

Grandmama used to say, "We're all right in our own eyes."
Younger me thought that meant I had to be right.
Now I know it means everyone's seeing through a cracked lens.
Sometimes love looks like letting people be.
So, I don't need to prove anything.
 I just want to live kind, hopeful, curious, considerate, and leave people better than I found them.
 Most evenings, Bart and I sit on the porch while the light fades.
We don't try to fix everything. We don't have to.
 Sometimes we talk; sometimes we let the quiet do the talking.
 We've been through love, loss, silence, storms, and after all these miles, we're still here.
 Not perfect. Present.
 For now, that's enough.
 You can rebuild a marriage the way you rebuild yourself—
piece by piece, choosing peace over pride, curiosity over control.
 I don't need fireworks. Bart can't be everything. I don't expect him to be.
 I take care of myself so when we come together, I'm as whole as I can be.
 We do it our way. It works.
 Give me quiet mornings, honest words, soft laughter, and someone to sit beside when the crickets start to sing. That's my love story now.
 Through every storm, I've been the wildflower—bending, growing through cracks and chaos, while Bart's been the steady oak. Different roots. Same weather. Still standing.
 Sometimes I think about the woman I used to be—half-asleep, hustling for worth, apologizing for being "too much," and somehow still never enough.
 If I could talk to her now, I'd say:
You don't have to earn rest.
You don't have to apologize for joy.
You don't have to explain why you need to be alone.
You're not running away anymore—you're coming home.

## The Backroads That Brought Me Home

Life isn't tidy.

It's wild and quiet, messy and magnificent, ordinary and divine.

I've cried on yoga mats, danced barefoot whenever the beat hit, prayed in deserts, and laughed until I cried.

Every bit of it brought me here.

At night, I don't pray for easy.

I pray for real moments where I'm fully awake, fully alive, fully me.

And if my time ever comes, let it be right here, on this porch, wrapped in my favorite shawl, sipping something green, writing words that might one day hand someone else a little more light.

Because I feel a change coming.

Good stuff. Fun stuff. Miracle stuff.

Road stuff and porch stuff.

The kind that feels like home.

Photo Credit: Michael Tarabay

## Five Things I Learned from the Roads That Brought Me Home

**1. Adventure doesn't always mean leaving—it means arriving.**
Sometimes the wildest trip you'll ever take is the one that leads you back to yourself.

**2. You can't outrun your own heart.**
I tried. God knows I tried. But the truth always catches up, and when it does, it comes gently—like waves rolling onto shore, whispering, "You're safe now."

**3. Travel changes you, but stillness transforms you.**
Being on the move opened my eyes. Sitting still opened my soul.

**4. Every place you love stays inside you.**
From Port A sunrises to Hill Country sunsets, the world keeps teaching me that beauty is not a destination—it's a way of seeing.

**5. Home isn't a house—it's peace.**
And sometimes, peace looks like a cup of coffee on the porch, wind in your hair, and the knowing that every twist in the road brought you right where you needed to be.

*Maybe resilience isn't about bouncing back; it's about learning to live beautifully changed.*

*The roads of resilience taught me how to breathe again.*
*The porch taught me how to rest.*

*It's morning coffee on the porch, deep breaths between thoughts, and dancing barefoot to live music because your body remembered joy before your brain did.*

*Peace isn't waiting for the world to quiet down; it's creating stillness right in the middle of the noise.*

*And that's what this whole road has been about: learning how to make peace in the middle of real life — wild, messy, beautiful, honest life.*

*Life finally started making sense to me as I emptied my soul on these pages. That's when the real road back to me began.* 11-1-25

# Final Note from the Road

If you've made it this far, thank you for riding shotgun.

I don't know what road you're on right now—maybe it's smooth, maybe it's full of potholes and detours you didn't see coming. But if my story proves anything, it's that even the roughest roads can still lead you home.

Here's what I know for sure: life's going to get messy. You'll cuss, you'll cry, you'll question everything—maybe even your sanity—but you'll keep going. Because that's what we do. You'll rebuild. You'll laugh again. You'll find peace in the middle of absolute chaos, and those tiny, quiet moments will save you.

Some days, peace looks like a sunrise and strong coffee on the porch. Other days, it's crying in your car with the AC blasting. Either way, you're still moving forward. Still breathing. Still here. And that counts.

If I could give you one piece of advice, it would be this: stop waiting for perfect. Perfect is a thief. Live now—messy, real, and beautifully human. Healing isn't about getting it all right; it's about showing up anyway. It's learning to laugh in the middle of the storm, to dance barefoot in the kitchen, to be grateful for whatever peace you can make today, even if it's small.

The backroads taught me that detours are the real path. The porch taught me that stillness matters. And life—with all its heartbreak, humor, and surprise—taught me that joy isn't something you find; it's something you create, right where you are.

So wherever you are tonight—on your porch, in your car, on your mat, or in your mess—take a deep breath. You're not lost. You're just on your way home.

I know, because I've been there too. I've spent years trying to find my own way back—back to peace, back to purpose, back to me. And funny enough, the trail started long before I ever knew it.

I've been writing since I was a kid, that girl with the spiral notebook full of doodles, song lyrics, and a carefully curated list of every boy I liked, complete with stars by their names. More stars meant a bigger

## Backroads and Backporches

crush. I took it very seriously. And somewhere on those pages, in my messy 12-year-old handwriting, was Bart's name.

I would've never guessed then—when I was just a girl scribbling dreams into a diary—that Bart would someday walk beside me through every chapter of my life, right up to this one. But that's the thing about life. Some roads you see coming from miles away. Others sneak up on you, twist when you least expect it, and take you places you never planned to go. Then one day, you look back and realize—it was always the road. Even the detours. Even the heartbreaks. Even the parts that made no sense at the time. They all led here.

Writing has always been how I make sense of it all. As a kid, it was diaries. As a teenager, it was letters I never sent. As an adult, it became stories, reflections, and half-finished thoughts scribbled in notebooks or typed into my phone. And somewhere along the way, photography joined the mix.

At first, it was just an outlet—a way to get outside, breathe, and remind myself that beauty still existed when life didn't feel beautiful. But over time, it became something more. Photography turned into meditation in motion—a kind of prayer without words. When I'm behind the lens, I'm still. I notice everything: the way light hits water, how wind moves through tall grass, how a sky can change moods faster than I can.

Eventually, I started printing my photos—Texas skies, coastal mornings, backroads glowing under stormy clouds—and hanging them in my home. I didn't realize it then, but I was decorating myself back to life. I'd walk past a print and catch myself breathing deeper, standing longer, just looking. Those photos became anchors, reminders that peace wasn't something out there waiting to be found. It could live right here, on my walls.

Later, I learned there was science behind it. In The Nature Fix, Florence Williams writes about how nature—even just images of it—can calm our nervous systems, lower stress hormones, and make us feel more alive. Hospitals, therapy offices, and healing spaces use nature art for that reason. Turns out, beauty and stillness don't just inspire us—

# Final Note From the Road

they heal us.

That realization changed everything. What started as therapy became art. What became art turned into a business. That's how Backroads and Backporches was born—not just as a name, but as a way of life. I wanted to share the peace I'd found in those quiet, ordinary places. Every photograph I take carries a little piece of that stillness—a reminder that we can come home to ourselves even in the middle of chaos.

When people hang my art in their homes, they're not just buying a photo—they're creating a space that breathes. Because the truth is, art changes how a room feels. It changes how we feel. You don't just look at it; you feel it in your body—the small shift when your shoulders drop, when your thoughts pause for a moment, when your eyes land on something that makes you remember what peace feels like.
That's what I hope my work does: remind people to slow down, to notice, to take a breath, to know that beauty is still here, always has been, even when life feels heavy. If you ever hang one of my photographs on your wall, I hope it gives you what it's given me: calm, clarity, and a little more room to breathe.

Peace shouldn't be rare or reserved. It should hang in our homes, live in our everyday spaces, and meet us in the moments we forget we need it most.

You can find my work, stories, and collections at www.backroadsandbackporches.com, or wander with me on Instagram @BackroadsandBackporches, where every photo has a story and every story leads back to a road worth remembering.
I don't know where the road ahead leads—and honestly, that's part of the fun now. But I do know this: I'll keep writing. I'll keep paying attention. I'll keep showing up. Because if life has taught me anything, it's that the point isn't to reach the destination—it's to stay awake for the drive.

If you ever find yourself standing at a crossroads wondering where to go next, remember—you're not alone. We're all out here on our own backroads, trying to find our way home.

## Backroads and Backporches

So here's to the journey. To love and loss. To laughter and lessons written in the dust. To all the crooked paths that somehow lead us exactly where we're supposed to be.

And here's to what's ahead—whatever it may be. Because this? This isn't the end. It never is.

Now go write your story—whether you ever share it or not. Write it for yourself. Revisit the child you were, the teenager finding her way, the twenty-something figuring life out, and every version that came after. You'll be amazed by what you discover—and you might just bring back some of the parts of you that you loved most.

Because home isn't always a place you find.

Sometimes, it's the story you finally tell.

Backroads and Backporches — they both have a way of bringing us home.

It would make a beautiful, cinematic fade-out for the last page.

# Acknowledgments

First and foremost, to Bart, the man whose name had stars by it when I was twelve. You've seen every version of me: the dreamer, the fighter, the crier, the dancer, the mess. You've built more than porches and decks; you've helped build a life that's weathered every kind of storm. Thank you for standing firm when I blew like a wildflower in a West Texas wind.

To my kids, Breanna, Noah, and Skyler, you are my greatest adventures. You've taught me more about love, acceptance, and laughter than any book or therapist ever could. You are the reason I keep growing, keep showing up, and keep trying to live as loudly and authentically as I hope you will. You're my proudest work of art.

To my family, the ones who stayed, the ones who left, and the ones I had to love from a distance, thank you. You've each shaped me in ways I'm still uncovering. Some lessons were hard, but every single one made me stronger, wiser, and more compassionate.

To my friends, the porch-sitters, road-trippers, soup-night regulars, art lovers and the ones who showed up when life fell apart, you're the real MVPs. Thank you for laughing with me, crying with me, and never once judging my questionable snack choices or my mid-story tangent detours.

To my therapist, for holding space, asking the hard questions, and introducing me to brownies with purpose. You helped me unearth truths that nearly broke me but ultimately set me free.

To Elmo, my loyal sidekick — thank you for being my co-pilot, my comfort, my calmer and the furry little reminder that unconditional love doesn't need words.

To the readers who found something of themselves in these pages — I see you. Writing this book cracked me open in ways I didn't expect, but if it permits even one person to breathe deeper, to speak their truth, or to take the long way home, then every word was worth it.

And finally, to the road itself — the highways, the dirt paths, the ones that ended in nowhere and the ones that led me straight to myself — thank you. You taught me that healing isn't linear, that detours are divine (okay, maybe not divine, but definitely necessary), and that peace is never out there waiting to be found. It's made right here, mile by mile, moment by moment.

Here's to the backroads and the backporches — and to all of us learning, in our own messy, beautiful ways, how to come home.

xoxo,

*Desiree Steele*

# ABOUT THE AUTHOR

Photo Credit: Michael Tarabay

For Desiree Steele, every road is a story, and every person is a world worth understanding. She is a documenter of human life—not just through her camera, but through the conversations, the quiet pauses, the laughter over coffee (always coffee), and the unexpected connections that happen when we actually slow down enough to listen. Desiree believes the most powerful stories are written by ordinary people living honest lives, and she is committed to seeing life through their eyes, not just her own.

Her work follows the roads that lead to people—their cultures, their resiliency, their way of loving and hurting, their healing, and their hope. Whether she is photographing the Texas Hill Country, sharing a meal with strangers, or traveling across the world, Desiree seeks to learn how others live and what they carry on their own backroads.

This calling is now taking her far beyond Texas. As a documenting photographer, she will be traveling to Portugal to capture a yoga retreat and walk alongside others on the Camino to Santiago, witnessing their transformations on ancient paths where every step is a prayer and every traveler is a teacher. With each story she encounters, she gathers what matters: the humanity we share, the faith we question, and the beauty we sometimes forget to see in ourselves.

Backroads and Backporches: The Road Back to Me is only the beginning. Desiree plans to continue writing, photographing, and honoring the lives she encounters—creating a series of books that celebrate real people and the roads that shape them. Because to her, storytelling isn't about spotlighting herself; it's about illuminating the truth and beauty found in others and sharing what she learns along the way.

## Want More Backroads and Backporches?

See Desiree Steele's collection of photos for sale, short stories, and up-coming events at:

🌐 **www.backroadsandbackporches.com**

📷 **@BackroadsandBackporches.**

◉ **@BackroadsandBackporches**

www.ingramcontent.com/pod-product-compliance
Lightning Source LLC
Chambersburg PA
CBHW071206110526
43967CB00084B/39